OUR HOLY FAITH
A RELIGION SERIES for THE ELEMENTARY SCHOOL

TEACHER'S MANUAL for

To Live is Christ

Based on the second half of the
Revised Baltimore Catechism
(Confraternity Edition)

ST. AUGUSTINE ACADEMY PRESS
HOMER GLEN, ILLINOIS

Nihil obstat:
    JOHN F. MURPHY
    Censor librorum

Imprimatur:
    + WILLIAM E. COUSINS
    Archbishop of Milwaukee
    May 17, 1961

This book was originally published in 1961
by Bruce Publishing, Milwaukee.

CONTENTS

GENERAL INTRODUCTION FOR THE SERIES

OUR HOLY FAITH

The Series, OUR HOLY FAITH, is intended to provide a complete, integrated, and basic course in religion for the eight grades of the elementary school.

The purpose of teaching religion in the elementary school is to see to it that the pupil has a clear and adequate knowledge of his holy Faith, so as to guide and influence his will to use grace in forming the image of Christ in himself. While primarily addressed to the intellect, it does not neglect the will or the child's attitudes and emotions. The first purpose of this religion Series, therefore, is clear and adequate knowledge of the Catholic religion.

The psychological basis for this is to be found in St. Augustine's little gem, "On Catechizing the Unlettered."*

St. Augustine tells us that in teaching religion we must lead the pupil from faith, to hope, to charity. The first step, therefore, is knowledge of our religion based on supernatural faith. The child is taught and accepts what Christ's Church, through her representative, proposes to be believed.

Content and Arrangement of the Series — Grades 1 and 2

The content of the first two grades is the traditional content of those grades, with emphasis on Confession and Holy Communion in the second grade.

Grades 3, 4, and 5

The first two grades are followed by two cycles of three grades each — 3 to 5 and 6 to 8. In Grades 3, 4, and 5, the No. 1 Baltimore Catechism is followed in the exact sequence of its lessons and indeed of its questions, in such fashion, however, that the first half of the No. 1 Revised Baltimore Catechism** (the Creed and the first three Commandments) is covered in the first book of that sequence (GOD'S TRUTHS HELP US LIVE); the second half of the No. 1 Catechism is covered in the third book of that sequence (LIVING LIKE CHRIST IN CHRIST). The second book of that sequence (THE VINE AND THE BRANCHES) is devoted to a study of the liturgy and the liturgical year. In this book the catechetical approach is, for obvious reasons, omitted. We have placed this material, which deals with an important area of religious

* There are many translations; that of Rev. Joseph P. Christopher, *De Catechizandis Rudibus* (Washington, D. C.: Catholic University, 1926), is very good.

** All references to the Catechism are to the Confraternity Edition.

instruction omitted in the Catechism, between two books devoted to explaining the Catechism.

Thus, the suggested sequence for Grades 3 to 5 is:

Grade 3 — GOD'S TRUTHS HELP US LIVE
(First half of No. 1 Catechism)

Grade 4 — THE VINE AND THE BRANCHES
(The liturgy and the liturgical year)

Grade 5 — LIVING LIKE CHRIST IN CHRIST
(Second half of No. 1 Catechism)

One value of this sequence is that it provides a change from the Catechism, applying the same doctrines but in a completely different manner.

Grades 6, 7, and 8

The books for the three remaining grades — 6, 7, and 8 — are similarly organized. In the first book of the sequence, OUR FAITH: GOD'S GREAT GIFT, the pupil studies the first half of the No. 2 Revised Baltimore Catechism. The second half of the No. 2 Catechism is then taken up in the volume, TO LIVE IS CHRIST, which is recommended for Grade 8 because it contains a review of the first half of the No. 2 Catechism and an intense study of its second half. The third book in this sequence (recommended for Grade 7, but usable in any grade from the sixth to the eighth) is entitled CHRIST IN PROMISE, IN PERSON, AND IN HIS CHURCH. It contains a complete chronological treatment of Bible History and of Church History, which have often been neglected in recent courses of study. The suggested sequence for Grades 6 to 8 is this:

Grade 6 — OUR FAITH: GOD'S GREAT GIFT
(First half of No. 2 Catechism)

Grade 7 — CHRIST IN PROMISE, IN PERSON, AND IN HIS CHURCH
(Bible History — Church History)

Grade 8 — TO LIVE IS CHRIST
(Second half of No. 2 Catechism)

Flexibility of the Series

Although the Series follows the sequence of the Catechism, its subject matter is so arranged that it is possible for a superintendent, a pastor, or a principal to adapt it to almost every course of study for religion in the elementary grades, or vice versa, to adapt the course of study to fit the Series. Since it contains books that are devoted to a study of the liturgy and of biblical and Church history, the Series makes it possible for the teacher to break up the monotony that frequently results from studying nothing but the Catechism year after year.

It is suggested that the book covering the first half of the No. 1 Catechism be used in Grade 3 and that the one dealing with the second half be employed for Grade 5, with the book on the liturgy for Grade 4. However the order of sequence can be changed if another order seems more appropriate. The book on the liturgy, THE VINE AND THE BRANCHES, can be postponed to Grade 5 if it is thought too difficult for Grade 4 (it is, however, no more difficult than science or geography in that grade); or it can be anticipated in an earlier grade or even completely omitted. The latter possibility, however, is one which the authors hope is not considered. Our present courses of study in elementary religion almost universally omit an ordered and intensive study of the liturgy and the liturgical year, which, as Pope Pius XII reminded us, is a basic means of religious instruction.

Method of Handling the Catechism

In the past, the method of teaching religion in the elementary schools was, quite justly, criticized for its misuse of the Catechism. The fault certainly did not lie in the Catechism, which is intended as a concise and precise synopsis of religious knowledge. The Catechism is designed to be studied carefully *after* it has been taught and explained authoritatively in the name of the Church.

Too often, however, the authoritative teaching and presentation have been omitted, and the child has been led directly to the bald, synoptic questions and answers of the Catechism, which he has been directed to study before or without any explanation and then repeat in rote fashion after he has memorized them.

Fortunately, in most modern courses of study in religion this abuse has been eliminated. The result has been courses of study more enjoyable to teacher and pupil alike.

Unfortunately, in many instances, the Catechism has also been abandoned. Bishops and pastors have deplored this, with great justification. An ordered knowledge of one's religion is absolutely necessary, and this the Catechism insures.

In this Series we have retained the exact sequence of the Catechisms No. 1 and No. 2. However, we have taken care to teach the content of the lessons *before* asking the child to study and, if necessary, to memorize the Catechism questions and answers. Thus we hope we have met the reasonable desires of the clergy, by accenting the Catechism, while not forgetting the needs and problems of the pupils and teachers in the classroom.

In many instances, while following the Catechism, we have added points not covered in it but necessary either as matters of knowledge or as material aiding assimilation and application of the basic doctrines. Our intention has been to make the study of religion as attractive and enjoyable and as instructive as possible. In short, we believe that a child's attitude toward religion is as important as his knowledge. One without the other is not of much value, and in this Series we have sought to integrate the two.

In this connection, however, let it be clearly stated and understood that the child's inclination or enjoyment is not the prime factor to be considered. We are dealing here with a matter that is not subject to the likes or dislikes of the pupil. Here we are concerned with a divinely constituted body of knowledge which the Church has a mandate to convey to the human race, and particularly to her members, in an authoritative way. "As the Father has sent me, I also send you. Going therefore . . ." (Mt. 28:28).

Here a curriculum determined by child interest or enjoyment would be an absurdity.

A Key Point — The Answer Before the Question

In the four years in which the texts of the Series are based directly on the Catechism — Grades 3, 5, 6, and 8 — we have included the Catechism answers in the body of the lessons, using the exact words of the Catechism; but we have expanded, paraphrased, and otherwise explained the meaning of the Catechism; this will insure that the child understands what the Catechism means, and will assist him to learn it when he studies the Catechism questions and answers at the end of the lesson. *The Catechism answers have been placed in boldface or in italics* to call attention to them. Thus, we teach the answer before we ask the child to learn it. The result is *understanding*, not mere rote memorization.

BASIC PRINCIPLES IN TEACHING RELIGION

What follows are the essential and fundamental principles for the teaching of religion. All else is accidental.

Begin With Faith

The first objective of the teaching of religion is a knowledge of the truths God wants us to know, and an acceptance of those truths on the basis of God's veracity — namely, an informed but unhesitating faith.

End With Love

The supreme objective of the teaching of religion, however, is not faith but love — love of God. The objective we have had in building this Series, and the objective the teachers of religion must have in teaching it, is to lead the pupil to a supernatural love of God.

With St. Augustine we ask every teacher of this Series to refer everything she teaches to the love of

God — God's love for us as proved by what He has done for us, and our love of God as proved by how we serve God in Himself and in our neighbors.

With God's love for us and ours for Him ever in mind, the teacher should present the doctrines and moral precepts of the Catholic religion in such a fashion that they lead the child first to an appreciation of his faith and a strengthening of that virtue in him; then to an increase of hope in him, for without supernatural hope there will be no continued striving.

The end, however, is love. The pupil should be led to see in everything that God has done an evidence of His love for us. He has loved us enough to reveal to us what He wants us to believe. He has revealed His existence, the incarnation, the redemption, the Church, the sacraments, the moral code we follow, the rewards He has in store for us, and so many other matters. In each of these truths He is proving His love for us. They should be so taught that, in all, God's love of us may stand out and arouse a desire to return love for love.

If truths are so taught, it will be easy for the child to see his obligation to love and serve God in return. They will not then be merely abstract truths with little personal meaning, but will become knowledge charged with motives for the will to requite that divine love.

Method and Content Intertwined

From the above it will be seen that method and content in the proper teaching of religion are closely intertwined. The point to be learned is first presented to the intellect as an object of faith and knowledge, then related to hope, as being possible, and finally to love as being something to be desired and possessed. All other details of methodology should be subordinated to this basic sequence.

It is all the more necessary to insist on this because the unit method we have used is also commonly employed in teaching the social studies. There, however, it is not based on supernatural virtues, but on the natural intellectual virtues.

Christian Formation

The formation of the perfect Christian, whose life is patterned on the life of Christ, is our final goal. This cannot be achieved by teaching or by the school. It is a supernatural task, requiring supernatural means. These means are in the possession of the Church. All the teacher can do is instruct and influence the pupil to fulfill his destiny as a member of Christ's Mystical Body, to see his role in the sacrifice it offers to the heavenly Father, to utilize the channels of grace it offers him. Solid, accurate, and full instruction by the teacher means much, but it does not guarantee the co-operation of the student. He still has his free will. The teacher can instruct, give good example, and pray — in doing these she does much. The home, too, can do much. But the grace of God, the Church and her means of grace, and the free will of the individual are all-important. We must do our utmost to enlighten the intellect and train the will of our charges — then leave the rest to God.

INTRODUCTION FOR TEACHER'S MANUAL TO ACCOMPANY
TO LIVE IS CHRIST

This *Manual* has been prepared for use with To Live Is Christ, Book 8 in the Religion Series Our Holy Faith. The doctrinal truths taught in this grade include the Creed, the Commandments, and the Means of Grace. Since the Creed and the first three Commandments of God are taught in Book 6 of the series, they are simply reviewed in Grade Eight. The last seven Commandments of God, the Commandments of the Church, and the Means of Grace are retaught at this higher grade level with added information and a new presentation.

In organization, content, and method the text attacks directly the primary objective of the teaching of religion — *Christlike living*. This objective is to give the pupils a knowledge of God and His eternal truths which will motivate them to lead Christlike lives.

THE TEXTBOOK

A careful study of To Live Is Christ discloses the following significant features:

1. It presents to the student in developed form the doctrinal truths contained in the revised edition of the Baltimore Catechism No. 2 (Confraternity edition).

The teachings of our Faith must be formulated very precisely. The catechism does this. But the teaching of these truths involves more than the memorization of catechetical formulas. The question-and-answer method and memorizing have a place in the teaching of religion, but only after the pupils have been taught what the catechism questions take for granted.

2. Throughout the text there is constant correlation with Sacred Scripture and Church History.

3. An attempt has been made to use pedagogical and psychological methods which recognize age, level of maturity, and interest of the child so as to make the study of religion attractive, vital, and effective.

4. Tests which follow each unit of work provide for measuring the pupil's progress.

THE UNITS

The textbook is divided into five major units and subunits under these. Thus, the content is divided into smaller sections, which can be more easily understood by the child. The introduction to each unit gives in outline form the material covered therein. ("Unit" is used to designate both the principal units and the subunits.)

ARRANGEMENT

In general, the material of each teaching unit in this Manual is arranged somewhat as follows:

I. Objectives of the Unit
A. Primary Objective
B. Auxiliary Objectives:
  For the intellect
  For the will

II. Introducing the Unit
(Sometimes combined with III, below.)

III. Notes on Teacher Presentation
  A. Suggestions for Developing Understanding of Subject Matter
  B. Correlating Activities
  C. Application

IV. Evaluation

V. Answers to End-of-Unit Tests in Textbook and Answers to Problems for Discussion

EXPLANATION OF HEADINGS USED IN THIS MANUAL

I. Objectives of the Unit

A. **Primary Objective.** The cement that binds the parts of a unit together, making it truly a unit, is its main objective. All that is included within the unit should converge upon that objective as a means toward an end. An effort has been made to state the primary objective as clearly and precisely as possible.

B. **Auxiliary Objectives.** The auxiliary objectives of each unit have been grouped under headings, "For the Intellect" and "For the Will." This is to impress teachers with the significance of both aspects of religious education, and to discourage the tendency to teach merely for understanding. Some of these objectives cannot be obtained without having recourse to the sacraments and prayer.

II. Introducing the Unit

The psychological value of setting the stage, as it were, for the learning process is well understood by all educators and needs no detailed explanation here.

III. Notes on Teacher Presentation

This section is merely suggestive. Teachers may be familiar with many of the ideas presented. However, much of this material will help teachers make their classes come alive and hold student interest. The suggestions are based on the personal experience of many teachers in religion. They are not intended to hamper teachers in the exercise of their own initiative and ingenuity, but to help them to organize their work and to present new and interesting material to pupils.

The activities suggested are intended as means to a single goal, namely, the vigorous, precise, and lively presentation of religious truths.

A. Suggestions for Developing an Understanding of Subject Matter. These include a wide variety of teaching techniques, such as word and phrase study, discussion problems, research activities, Scripture hunts, and questions.

B. Correlating Activities. These are suggested to show the pupils how they can enhance the knowledge they gain in their religion class by relating it to other activities, both at school and away.

C. Application. Since the goal of religious instruction is not purely speculative knowledge about the truths of faith but moral action based on such knowledge, it has been thought advisable to indicate various ways for putting the truths learned in religion class to work in daily life.

IV. Evaluation

Additional tests are provided in the *Manual* to supplement those contained in the text proper. The teacher may make use of or disregard these additional tests according to her judgment of the needs of her class.

V. Answers to Study Exercises in Textbook and Answers to Problems for Discussion

The Manual offers the answers to Study Exercises so that the task of correcting pupils' work will be made less burdensome.

METHOD AND LESSON PLANS

The Eighth Grade book is written with the hope that it will be taught on the Unit Method. This implies generally that each unit shall have a lesson or more as Launching, Introduction, Presentation, or whatever you wish to call the initial presentation of the new ideas and the associating of them with the preceding unit or previous knowledge. A brief check on existing knowledge of the subject can be included.

This will be followed by Study-Work Periods of various types as the matter requires, for instance: Development Lessons, presenting and developing new material; Directed Study Lessons (with questions or assignments controlling the direction of what is to be studied); Supervised Study Lessons (in which the teacher assigns the topic or topics, the question or questions, etc., and supervises by circulating around the room); Drill Lessons; Discussion Lessons; and Appreciation Lessons. The unit will be ended with a Culmination Lesson or Lessons. These can take many forms, organizing the material of the unit orally, in written organized form, in a project, etc. Finally, an Evaluation Lesson, with any necessary reteaching or drilling, will conclude the unit.

Some sample lesson plans illustrating the types of lessons just described follow.

SAMPLE LESSON PLANS

These sample lessons are based on specific matter from the textbook. The plans apply to one particular phase or type of work which should be carried out within each unit. The sample plans which follow can be used as guides for preparing similar lesson plans for other units and sections.

The following are the plans which are here presented:
Sample Development Lesson Plan
Sample Directed Study Lesson
Sample Supervised Study Lesson
Sample Discussion Lesson
Sample Drill Lesson
Sample Appreciation Lesson
Sample Culmination Lesson
Other examples can be found in other *Teacher's Manuals* of this Series.

SAMPLE LESSON PLAN FOR DEVELOPMENT LESSON

UNIT III:

Living Through Christ, With Christ, In Christ

SECTION IV:

Christ Gives Us Himself in Holy Communion Through the Sacrifice of the Mass.

(Text, *To Live Is Christ*, pp. 262–266)

SUBJECT MATTER:

The Mass of the Faithful . . . "We Sacrifice" (pp. 262–266)

TYPE:

Development

OBJECTIVES:

A. To develop greater appreciation of and love for the Mass

B. To realize the meaning of the prayers offered during the Canon.

C. To awaken a longing for active participation in the Mass, especially at the Consecration.

MATERIALS:

Mass photos

A Missal

Diagrams of the parts of the Mass on the blackboard or bulletin board

PROCEDURE:

A. Approach

Show the pupils a photograph picturing an altar with tabernacle and crucifix above the tabernacle. Begin a discussion with them to see if anyone from the group can say why a crucifix is associated with the tabernacle. From the discussion which follows lead the pupils to an understanding that the Sacrifice of the Mass is the same as the Sacrifice of the Cross, and that the sacrificial part of the Mass is the center of the entire act of worship.

B. Presentation and Explanation

Here take up, point by point, the actions performed by priest and faithful at Mass from the beginning of the Canon to the Minor Elevation. This could be carried out in the following steps:

1. *Introduction:* The priest intones the *Dominus vobiscum* to begin the Preface, inviting the faithful to join with him in offering the Sacrifice. It is a reminder that we are coming to the very heart of the Mass. The priest reminds us how we are to be disposed ("Lift up your hearts") and of the theme of the Mass ("Let us give thanks to the Lord our God").

2. *The Preface Itself:* During this prayer we offer thanks to God the Father, through His Son and our Lord, Jesus Christ, and together with His angels. The spirit of the Preface is revealed in this thankful adoration of the Father through His Son. It concludes with two ancient chants:
   a) The *Sanctus,* the prayer of praise offered by the angels; and
   b) The *Benedictus,* the prayer of the people of Jerusalem offered on Palm Sunday.

3. *Prayer to Accept the Offering:* The Father is asked to accept the sacrifice offered through His Son for the salvation of the world ("We therefore humbly pray . . .").

4. *Remembrance Prayers Before the Consecration:* In striking fashion, the prayers offered to the Father before the Consecration show us how much the Mass is the sacrificial act of Christ's Mystical Body, His Church, for these prayers are offered in behalf of the Church militant, and in union with the Church Triumphant.

5. *Offering Prayers Before the Consecration:* Next follow two prayers: the first asks God to accept our sacrifice and, in return, to grant us peace, salvation, and sanctity; the second implores Him to bless, accept, and perfect our offering.

6. *Consecration:* The bread and wine are here changed into the living Christ through the ministry of His priest.

7. *Offering Prayers After the Consecration:* The three prayers following the Consecration:
   a) Recall that the Victim offered in the Mass is the same as that of Calvary,
   b) Liken it to the sacrifices of Abel, Abraham, and Melchisedech in the Old Testament, and
   c) Call down heavenly blessings on those who offer this Sacrifice.

8. *Remembrance Prayers:* Next priest and faithful beg God to be mindful of the Church Suffering, the Church Militant, and all created nature.

9. *Conclusion:* These prayers are followed by the "Minor Elevation" in which the Three Persons of the Trinity are addressed and in which the union between Christ and His faithful is stressed.

C. Summary

Using the Mass chart or photographs of the Mass, direct the pupils to tell one fact about the parts of the Canon.

D. Application

Have the pupils reflect on the following:
   "All that He has, all that He is, He gives.
   All that we have, all that we are, He takes."
Elicit some practices that could be derived from today's lesson. Have pupils make their own resolutions.

E. Assignment

Make a list of all the new prayers and terms learned in today's lesson. Define each.
Read and report on one of the sacrifices of the Old Law (Abel, Abraham, Melchisedech).

SAMPLE LESSON PLAN FOR DIRECTED STUDY LESSON

UNIT III:

Living Through Christ, With Christ, In Christ

SECTION IV:

Christ Gives Us Himself in Holy Communion Through the Sacrifice of the Mass.

(Text, *To Live Is Christ*, pp. 254–257)

SUBJECT MATTER:

The Holy Sacrifice of the Mass . . . "We Speak to God."

Mass of Preparation

TYPE:

Directed Study

OBJECTIVES:

A. To learn the significance of the parts of the Mass . . . "We Pray."

B. To increase knowledge and appreciation for these parts.

C. To encourage an active participation in the Mass through the use of a Missal.

MATERIALS:

Missal
Catechism . . . The New Baltimore Catechism No. 2
Mass chart

PROCEDURE:

A. Approach

If all the 1,600,000,000 people in the world stood on each other's shoulders, thus forming one gigantic individual, such a giant would be ten billion feet tall, or almost two million miles high. Standing on the earth he could look down at the moon, which would scarcely reach above his ankles. The sun over his ear would be no higher than forty-six times his own height.

B. Presentation

Yet, such a giant would never be as mighty as a little child on its knees reaching to God through prayer. And when it is the greatest prayer in the Church — the Mass, what power it possesses to move the Heart of God! Is it any wonder then that the first part of the Mass of Preparation is "We Pray"?

C. Directed Study

1. Why is the Mass of Preparation called the Mass of the Catechumens? (Text, p. 254; Missal, pages will vary.)
2. Why does the priest make the sign of the cross when beginning prayers at the foot of the altar? (Text, p. 254.)
3. What should we do when the priest makes the sign of the cross? (Text, p. 254.)
4. The next prayer is one of joy. Find it and read it from your Missal. Discuss the meaning of it. "I will go unto the Altar of God . . ." (Text, p. 254; Missal.)
5. What is the translation for *Judica Me?* What does this psalm recall? (Text, p. 254; Missal.)
6. To approach God's altar we must be pure of heart. In which prayer do we ask the heavenly court to intercede for us? Read it from your Missal. (Text, p. 255; Missal.)
7. What phrases in the *Confiteor* prove that this is a public confession? (Text, 255; Missal.)
8. Ascending the altar the priest goes to the Missal and gives the keynote for the day's feast. Which prayer is this? Read this prayer from today's Proper. (Text, p. 256; Missal.)
9. Returning to the middle of the altar the priest recites the *Kyrie*. What is this prayer? To whom is it addressed? What feeling does it express? (Text, p. 256.)
10. We then join the priest in a hymn of praise. What is this prayer? When was it first sung? (Text, p. 256; Missal.)
11. The priest greets the people with *Dominus vobiscum*. What does this mean? How does it apply to us? (Text, p. 256; Missal.)
12. Next is the official prayer for the day's feast. What is it called? How does it end? Read the Collect from your Missal for today's feast. What application can you derive? (Text, p. 256; Missal.)

D. Summary

We Pray

Prayers at the foot of the altar . . . . . Sorrow
Introit (Theme) . . . . Keynote
Kyrie . . . . Ninefold plea for mercy
Gloria . . . Hymn of praise to all Three Persons
Collect . . . . Prayer of petition

E. Application

Somewhere in the world a priest is about to offer the Holy Sacrifice of the Mass. In spirit let us unite ourselves with all the Masses that are being offered all over the world. With the priest let us express sorrow for all of our sins, and resolve to do better in the future.

Say the *Confiteor*.

F. Assignment

Study the outline on "We Pray." Know a statement or two about each prayer. Be able to arrange the prayers in sequence.

Report on a parable exemplifying one of the following: sorrow, mercy, perseverance, hope, praise.

SAMPLE LESSON PLAN FOR A SUPERVISED STUDY LESSON

UNIT III:

Living Through Christ, With Christ, In Christ

SECTION IV:

Christ Gives Us Himself in Holy Communion Through the Sacrifice of the Mass.

(Text, *To Live Is Christ*, pp. 260–262)

SUBJECT MATTER:

The Mass of the Faithful . . . "We Offer." From the Offertory Verse to the Secret Prayer.

TYPE:

Supervised Study

OBJECTIVES:

A. To further our knowledge of the meaning of the Mass.

B. To increase love of Christ in our hearts because of His great gift to man . . . the Mass.

MATERIALS:

See Procedure B, 5, below.

PROCEDURE:

A. Approach

Read the following poem and discuss:

"Not what we give but what we share,
For the gift without the giver is bare,
Who gives himself with his alms feeds three . . .
Himself, his hungering neighbor, and Me."

B. Presentation

1. Topic for study:
"We Offer" . . . from the Offertory Verse to Secret Prayer.

2. Points to help study the topic:
   The Offertory Verse and the Offering of the Bread
   a) What actions of our Lord at the Last Supper are reproduced in the Offertory?
   b) How many prayers are included in the Offertory? Which of these prayers are always the same? Were these prayers always part of the Mass? What took their place for a long time?
   c) Our gift to God is really ourselves under the symbols of bread and wine. Discuss.
   Mixing of the Water and Wine . . . Prayer to the Holy Spirit.
   d) What was lacking in the sacrifice Cain offered? What must we therefore do about offering the Mass?
   e) What conclusion will you draw from the fact that the pronoun "I" is seldom used in the Mass?
   f) What significance does the mixing of the water and the wine have?
   g) After having said the prayer of the offering, the priest then says a prayer of humility. Why?
   h) Why is the Holy Spirit invoked during the Offertory part of the Mass?
   Washing of the Hands . . . Secret Prayers
   i) Why is incense used at church services?
   j) How does the use of incense show that our prayers must come from a heart on fire with love?
   k) Why is it that all who assist at a solemn Mass are incensed?
   l) The washing of hands at the Mass is both necessary and symbolic for the priest. Why?
   m) What lesson does the washing of hands imply for the congregation attending the Mass?
   n) In what way does the *Orate Fratres* bring out the laity's share in the Sacrifice? Show that this same prayer stresses what should be the foremost purpose of all our praying.
   o) Why is the last of the Offertory prayers called the *Secret?*
   p) What evidence can you find in your Missal that we all offer the Mass with the priest?
   q) What incidents of our Lord's life can you associate with the actions and prayers of the priest at the Offertory part of the Mass?

3. Word development:

Orate Fratres	*Lavabo*
congregation	Offertory
laity	incense

4. Standards:
Elicit the standards to be followed during the independent study.
   a) Use the time allotted wisely.
   b) Work neatly.
   c) Be sure to include the sources of information.

5. Materials for individual study:
   a) *Know Your Mass* . . . Catechetical Guild
   b) The Daily Missal
   c) *The Ceremonies of the Mass*
   d) Textbook

C. Evaluation

Check pupils on the standards.

D. Application:

Have pupils unite themselves with the Masses that are being said throughout the world.

Elicit from them examples of something they can resolve to do today so that their offering tomorrow at Mass will take on a deeper meaning.

E. Assignment:

Things to discuss and do, pp. 274–275.

SAMPLE LESSON PLAN FOR DISCUSSION LESSON

UNIT III:

Living Through Christ, With Christ, In Christ

SECTION IV:

Christ Gives Us Himself in Holy Communion Through the Sacrifice of the Mass.

(Text, *To Live Is Christ*, pp. 262–266)

SUBJECT MATTER:

The Mass of Sacrifice . . . "We Sacrifice"; the Canon

TYPE:

Discussion

OBJECTIVES:

A. To provide an opportunity for sharing ideas and information about the Canon obtained through reading.
B. To increase our love for the Mass and our desire for active participation, particularly at the solemn moment of Consecration.
C. To develop a desire to be transformed into Christ at the Consecration.

MATERIALS

Missal

Mass chart

Text

Mass photos

Personal Mass pamphlets

PROCEDURE:

A. Approach

God has given us the power of changing the bread we eat into our body and blood (Assimilation).

B. Presentation

Has He not also power to change bread and wine into His own Body and Blood? (Transubstantiation.)

C. Group Discussion

1. Set standards:
   a) Back up statements.
   b) Everyone participates.
2. Topic for discussion: "We Sacrifice" . . . the Canon
3. The following topics are suggested for Group I:
   Preface . . . Sanctus . . . Benedictus
   a) What does the dialogue that precedes the Preface bring to our minds?
   b) What is the theme of the Preface?
   c) When does the Preface of the Mass change?
   d) Where did the short prayers that follow the Preface originate? Explain them.

4. Topic for Group II:
   Remembrances . . . Offering Prayers
   a) What does the priest ask of God in the first short introductory prayer of the Canon? Why?
   b) Compare the three remembrance prayers that are said before the Consecration.
   c) Why does the priest place his hands over the bread and wine in the first offering prayer?
   d) This offering has a threefold purpose. Discuss.
   e) What is asked for in the second prayer?
5. Topic for Group III:
   Consecration
   a) What story is narrated?
   b) How does it differ from the telling of any other story?
   c) What is transubstantiation?
   d) What should we do at the moment of Consecration of bread and wine? What prayer should we say at the Elevation? Why?
6. Topic for Group IV:
   Offering Prayers . . . Remembrances
   a) Mention the Old Testament sacrifices recalled in this prayer. State the purpose of each.
   b) Does the second prayer mention anything about Holy Communion? Explain.
   c) Compare the three remembrance prayers said after the Consecration.
7. Topic for Group V:
   Little Elevation
   a) What is the Little Elevation?
   b) Why are the Host and Chalice raised together?
   c) What is the closing prayer for the Canon of the Mass? Why?

D. Class Discussion

The members of the class who did not participate in the group discussion ask questions of the discussion groups, and add important points they may wish to contribute.

E. Summary

1. Solemn introduction to the Canon:
   Preface
   Sanctus
   Benedictus
2. Remembrances:
   Church Suffering
   Church Militant
   Church Triumphant
3. Offering prayers:
   Prayer of atonement and petition for peace, safety of soul, and final perseverance.
4. Consecration:
   "This is My Body"
   "This is My Blood"

5. Elevation:
   "My Lord and My God"
6. Offering prayers:
   Thanksgiving and recalling Old Testament sacrifices: Abel, Melchisedech, Abraham.
   Preparation for Holy Communion
7. Remembrances:
   Church Suffering
   Church Militant . . . "We Sinners"
   All Nature
8. Minor Elevation
   Host and Chalice raised together to show how Christ offered His Body and Blood on the cross

F. Application

The high point of the Canon, of the Mass of Sacrifice, is the *Consecration*.
The following words are true. Can you give reasons, why they are? What do they teach us about the Mass? the Consecration?

"All that He has, all that He is, He gives.
All that we have, all that we are, He takes."

Private meditation asking Christ to transform us into Himself just as at Mass bread and wine undergo a transubstantiation.

G. Assignment

Make an acrostic on the word *Consecration* or *Canon*.

SAMPLE LESSON PLAN FOR A DRILL LESSON

UNIT III:

Living Through Christ, With Christ, In Christ

SECTION IV:

Christ Gives Us Himself in Holy Communion Through the Sacrifice of the Mass.
(Text, *To Live Is Christ*, pp. 247–266)

SUBJECT MATTER:

The Holy Sacrifice of the Mass . . . from the Prayers at the Foot of the Altar to the End of the Canon

TYPE:

Drill

OBJECTIVES:

A. To further the retention of material studied thus far.
B. To develop a greater love for the Mass as a result of a better understanding of its parts.

MATERIALS:

Drill devices prepared by the teacher

PROCEDURE:

A. Approach

Short discussion of slogan: "Love God and do as you please."

B. Presentation

In the study of the Mass we have learned that we have at our disposal the most powerful prayer. Nothing is more pleasing to God than this Holy Sacrifice. This lesson will show how well we have learned the parts of the Mass and, consequently, how well we shall be able to assist at Mass.

C. Drill Devices

Split Sentences (two teams): Team A reads the first part; Team B completes the statement.

1. The sacrifices of the Old Law were not perfect because *the victims were not perfect.*
2. When the priest changes bread and wine into the Body and Blood of Christ, he is fulfilling Christ's command, *"Do this in commemoration of me."*
3. One aim of the Liturgical Movement is that *the faithful acquire a better understanding of the sacrifice of the Mass.*
4. The Offertory procession, which once held a prominent place in the Mass of the Faithful, is *no longer found in the Mass.*
5. The priest kisses the altar at various times during the Mass *because it represents Christ.*
6. The Mass of Preparation is divided into two parts — *service of prayer and service of instruction.*
7. The Mass is the same Sacrifice as the Sacrifice of the Cross because *the Victim and the principal priest are the same.*
8. Mass is offered for four purposes: *adoration, contrition, thanksgiving, supplication.*
9. The prayers of remembrance before and after the consecration *gather the whole Church around the Sacrifice of Christ.*
10. In the Mass the offering of the Victim is made by *the priest, acting in the person of Christ and in the name of all the faithful.*
11. The Sacrifice of the Mass is *the highest form of public worship in the Catholic Church.*
12. The 42nd Psalm ("Give judgment for me, O God . . ."), which is said at the foot of the altar, reminds us *that sin makes us exiles from God, like King David.*
13. The Gospel in the Mass *is the most important part in the Mass of Preparation.*

14. Our self-offering to God in the Mass *is symbolized by the bread and wine used in the Offertory.*

15. In the Mass today, Christ does not suffer *because He offers His sacramental Body.*

16. We stand during the Gospel *because we want to show God that we honor and love His Word.*

17. The *Credo* is like the Act of Faith and the Apostles' Creed *because in each of them we tell God we believe in Him.*

18. The Oration (Collect) is a prayer which *asks God to give us what we need in order to serve Him better.*

19. The Preface is *a prayer of praise to God the Father.*

20. The highest purpose in offering the Sacrifice of the Mass is *the adoration of God.*

Flash Cards: Identification . . . one sentence about each term. Two teams have the same number of cards. A team forfeits a card when a member fails to give the correct answer. The team with the greater number of cards is the winner:

catechumen	*Kyrie*	Preface
Offertory	*Lavabo*	Tract
Transubstantiation	Epistle	*Gloria*
Dominus vobiscum	Proper	*Alleluia*
Benedictus	Amen	*Confiteor*
Munda cor meum	Credo	*Sanctus*
Ordinary	*Oremus*	Collect
sacrifice	Psalm 42	Introit
Sequence	Secret	Gospel
Gradual		

Interpreters: Number of words translated in 1 minute:

Confiteor	*Amen*
Oremus	*Gloria*
Munda cor meum	*Judica me*
Orate Fratres	*Lavabo*
Deo gratias	*Et cum spiritu tuo*
Sanctus	*Gloria tibi Domine*
Kyrie	*Credo*
Dominus vobiscum	*Lectio*
Per omnia saecula	*Sursum corda*

Beat the Clock (allow ½ minute): Arrange the prayers of the Mass in sequential order. Pick up any five cards from the chalk ledge. Arrange them quickly in proper sequence. Read the arrangement.

Quiz Master and Quiz Kids:
How does the Holy Spirit speak to us in the sermon?

Why do we say *Deo gratias* after the Epistle?

What is the original meaning of the word "Good-by"?

Why does the priest recite the Collect with hands extended?

What does the priest say before beginning the Collect? Why?

Why does the priest say the prayer of Isaias before beginning the Gospel?

Why is the Gradual placed after the Epistle?

Why do the people stand to hear the Gospel?

What is the difference between the Nicene Creed and the Apostles' Creed?

Why does the priest wash his hands at the *Lavabo*?

Explain why the Canon is called the "Heart of the Mass"?

Why are the three Old Testament characters mentioned in the first Offering Prayer after the Consecration?

Acrostic: Fill in the missing blanks from the word list (spelling check):

M a s s
A l l e l u i a
S e q u e n c e
S a c r i f i c e

I n t r o i t
S e r m o n

A m e n

S a n c t u s
A d o r a t i o n
C o l l e c t
R e m e m b r a n c e s
I n t r o i b o
F r a t r e s (*O r a t e*)
I m m o l a t i o n
C r e e d
E p i s t l e

D. Evaluation

Pupils evaluate lesson in the light of responses given. Decide whether the lesson proves that the material was well covered or if added time should be devoted to the study of the Mass.

E. Application

Listen to recording of the *Sanctus* of the Mass.

Short meditation on the *Sanctus*.

Pupils make their own resolution.

SAMPLE LESSON PLAN FOR AN APPRECIATION LESSON

UNIT III:

Living Through Christ, With Christ, In Christ

SECTION IV:

Christ Gives Us Himself in Holy Communion Through the Sacrifice of the Mass.
(Text, *To Live Is Christ*, pp. 247–277)

SUBJECT MATTER:

The Holy Sacrifice of the Mass

TYPE:

Appreciation

OBJECTIVES:

A. To develop greater appreciation and love for the Mass.
B. To increase the desire to communicate sacramentally at Mass.

MATERIALS:

Mass chart, *Maryknoll Magazine*, May, 1954

PROCEDURE:

1. Approach

Review movements of the Mass . . .

Going up to God   God coming down to us

We pray   We learn   We offer   We receive
Mass of Preparation   *Mass of Sacrifice*

How can we best assist at the Holy Sacrifice of the Mass? (*Answer:* Use a Missal, receive Holy Communion, be united with the priest.)

2. Reflection

Story . . . "The Little Martyr" (*Maryknoll Magazine*, May, 1954). Death comes from a Red's gun as a little girl gives herself her last earthly Holy Communion.

3. Affection

Although no Red soldier keeps me from assisting at Mass and Holy Communion, do I make use of the countless opportunities God has given me?

Is my desire for Christ in Holy Communion as intense as the girl's in the story?

Am I willing to undergo sacrifice and inconvenience in order to assist at Mass and receive Holy Communion?

How can I thank God sufficiently for the privileges I have in living in this country?

4. Application

Pupils recite the Mass Clock prayer, uniting themselves with Masses being offered all over the world.

Private prayer of thanksgiving and Spiritual Communion. Song: "O What Could My Jesus Do More."

5. Resolution

In gratitude for the Holy Mass resolve to assist more frequently and with greater devotion, and to communicate sacramentally . . . (each pupil decides for himself how often).

SAMPLE LESSON PLAN FOR A CULMINATION LESSON

UNIT III:

Living Through Christ, With Christ, In Christ

SECTION IV:

Christ Gives Us Himself in Holy Communion Through the Sacrifice of the Mass.
(Text, *To Live Is Christ*, pp. 228–290)

SUBJECT MATTER:

The Holy Sacrifice of the Mass

TYPE:

Culminating

OBJECTIVE:

To organize our understanding and develop a deeper appreciation of the Holy Sacrifice, in order to live the Mass in our daily life.

MATERIALS:

Records   Pictures
Charts   Written reports

PROCEDURE:

1. Song: Chant . . . *Sanctus*
2. Reporters: (two-minute floor talks)
   a) "To sacrifice is not to give up a thing, but rather to give it."

b) "It is the Mass that makes men men" (G. K. Chesterton).

c) "A Christian will become a saint if he earnestly lives the Liturgical Year."

3. Performers (Dramatizations):

a) Parable of the Sower *or*

b) Prodigal Son

4. Correspondents (letters):

a) To a convert . . . "The Mass is a drama in which each of us is an actor."

b) To a non-Catholic who contends, "We need not bother about any creed, but merely live a good life."

5. Interpreters (quotations . . . applications):

a) "All that He has, all that He is, He gives; all that we are, all that we have, He takes."

b) Ecclus. 25:2

6. Panelists (panel discussion):
Topic: "The Mass, the center of Catholic life in our parish."

7. Impersonators (saints in the Canon of the Mass)

8. Judges (have jury solve problems, offer suggestions for improvement)

9. Advertisers (explain charts, pictures, symbols)

10. Testers (challenge the class with a crossword puzzle based on the parts of the Mass)

11. Appreciation (listen to recordings of the Mass chants)

N.B. It is impossible to carry out all the activities mentioned above in a regular class period. This is just a sampling of enjoyable projects which may be carried out.

UNIT ONE. CHRIST TEACHES US THROUGH HIS CHURCH—A REVIEW

(Text, pp. 1–45)

OUTLINE OF CONTENT

I. What We Know About God
(Text, pp. 4–10; Baltimore Catechism [No. 2], Lessons 1–3)

II. God Created the Angels and Men
(Text, pp. 11–19; Baltimore Catechism, Lessons 4–6)

III. How God's Love Redeemed Man
(Text, pp. 20–26; Baltimore Catechism, Lessons 7–8)

IV. How the Graces of the Redemption Came to Us
(Text, pp. 27–39; Baltimore Catechism, Lessons 9–12)

V. The Last Four Articles of the Creed
(Text, pp. 40–45; Baltimore Catechism, Lessons 13–14)

TEACHING SUGGESTIONS FOR UNIT ONE

The teaching suggestions for this first unit are very brief because it is a review unit. Do not bore the students by hammering away at matter which most of them already know. Let the pupils do most of the talking in this unit. It will be good for them and revealing for you.

I. OBJECTIVES OF THE UNIT

A. Primary Objective
To review our knowledge of the necessity of faith for salvation and to encourage us to live the faith.

B. Auxiliary Objectives

For the Intellect:
1. To understand and appreciate the chief truths of faith contained in the Apostles' Creed.
2. To become acquainted with the teachings of Christ and to follow the example of His Life.
3. To increase our knowledge of the Holy Spirit, the Third Person of the Blessed Trinity, who dwells in the Church and sanctifies men through the gift of grace.

For the Will:
1. To appreciate the value of the gift (virtue) of faith, and the ways in which we use this gift.
2. To appreciate our membership in the Church, the Mystical Body of Christ.
3. To co-operate with our bishop and priests in spreading the Kingdom of Christ on earth.
4. To make use of the means of grace which Christ provides for us.

II. NOTES ON TEACHER PRESENTATION

A. Suggestions for Developing Understanding of Subject Matter
1. Use the filmstrip and recordings on the Creed.
2. Have a bulletin-board display of pictures of martyrs and missionaries, using a caption: "Witnesses to the Truth of God."
3. Consider Christ's command, "Going . . . teach" and its relation to Catholic schools and missions.
4. Use pictures from magazines and newspapers to discuss current events which call for heroic service to God.
5. Discuss: *One Faith, One Head, One Life in Christ.*

B. Correlating Activities
1. Write a letter to a non-Catholic friend who contends: "We need not bother about any creed, but merely live a good life."
2. Discuss: "This is the victory that overcomes the world, our faith."
3. Decorate the room in keeping with the theme of this unit. *Suggestions:* symbols of our Faith; pictures of saints or martyrs who professed their faith in God; illustrations from nature or science books pointing to the truth that God exists; illustrations of mission activities showing the work of missionaries.
4. Write a paragraph or compose a poem on one of the following topics:
   How I Can Spread the Word of God
   What My Faith Means to Me
   How We Can in Daily Life Profess Our Faith

5. Let each pupil bring to class an example of God's power or goodness or providence as seen in the everyday affairs of life.

6. Report on saints who have been active in promoting the cause of Christ: St. Peter, St. Paul, St. Augustine, St. Patrick, St. Boniface, etc.

7. Read the parables. Listen to their explanation. Choose some for illustration in a mural or series of panels: The Good Samaritan, The Unforgiving Servant, The Good Shepherd, The Rich Man and Lazarus, The Prodigal Son, The Sower and the Seed.

8. Analyze the hymn of praise, "Holy God We Praise Thy Name." Sing it with faith and devotion.

9. *Bible Hunt:* Find several stories in the Bible that illustrate the mercy, the love, or justice of God. Plan a TV program dramatizing the scenes.

10. Make a poster showing how the members of the Mystical Body are drawn from all nationalities, races, and conditions of men, united in Christ.

11. Relate incidents of angels acting as messengers of God to man.

12. Make a list of the indulgenced ejaculations in honor of the Father, Son, and Holy Spirit. Make it a practice to recite a few of them each day.

13. Make a study of your parish: the role of the priest, the sacramental life of the parish, the school, the societies.

III. EVALUATION

A. God the Father — Creator (additional material)

Completion: Complete the following statements by supplying the missing word. Place your answer in the column to the right.

1. The chief gift bestowed on Adam and Eve was (1).
2. We attribute the work of creation to God the (2).
3. God occasionally sent (3) as messengers to men.
4. The account of the creation of the world is given in the Bible, in the Book of (4).
5. The only human person ever preserved from original sin was the (5).
6. God the Father is the (6) Person of the Blessed Trinity.
7. God's care for man is called (7).
8. When we say the angels are pure spirits we mean they have no (8).
9. The likeness of God is chiefly in the (9).
10. After Adam fell into sin God promised to send a (10).

1. Sanctifying grace
2. Father
3. angels
4. Genesis
5. Blessed Virgin
6. First
7. Divine Providence
8. bodies
9. soul
10. Redeemer

B. God the Son — Our Redeemer

Completion: Do the same with the following exercise.

1. The Saviour of all men is (1).
2. Christ proved that He was God especially by His (2).
3. (3) means that Christ offered His sufferings and death as a fitting sacrifice in satisfaction for the sins of men and regained for mankind the right to heaven.
4. Because Christ pleads for us with the Father, He is called our (4).
5. I believe that Jesus Christ is the (5) Person of the Blessed Trinity, true (6) and (7) man.
6. By the (8) I mean that the Son of God was made man. The rewards Christ earned by His sufferings and death are called (9).
7. Christ rose from the dead to show that He is (10) and to teach us that we, too, shall (11) from the dead.
8. Christ left this earth on (12) Day.
9. The fact that Christ suffered proved that He was (13).

1. Jesus Christ
2. miracles
3. Redemption
4. Mediator
5. Second
6. God
7. true
8. Incarnation
9. merits
10. God
11. rise
12. Ascension
13. man

C. The Church

Can you give the answers for the following?

1. Do a French Catholic priest and an American Catholic priest always teach the same doctrines? Why?
2. Do kind acts such as giving food to hungry people help to spread the faith and save men's souls? Why?
3. "He who hears you, hears me. He who rejects you, rejects me." Why?
4. A "rubber conscience" is bad. Why?

Matching: Match Column A with Column B and print the letter of your choice in the answer blank on the right.

Column A	*Column B*	
1. It is natural for people	A. because it was founded by Christ on the Apostles.	1. E
2. The Catholic Church is apostolic	B. the Catholic Church is *catholic*.	2. A
3. Because it is for all people	C. until the end of time.	3. B
4. The Holy Spirit will dwell in the Church	D. the will of its divine Founder.	4. C
5. The Church always does	E. to look for truth to satisfy their minds.	5. D

D. The Mystical Body of Christ

Multiple choice: Choose the correct answer and print the letter of your choice in the answer space on the right.

1. The mediator between God and the members   1. C
   of a parish is the
   A. altar boy   C. priest
   B. lay Brother   D. Sister

2. By corporate worship is meant   2. D
   A. bodily worship   C. divine honor
   B. profound adoration D. group worship

3. The chief concern and interest of a parish is   3. D
   A. parish activities C. success in life
   B. financial success D. the divine life of grace

4. To forgive all injuries is a spiritual work of   4. B
   mercy because it
   A. relates to the relief of bodily wants
   B. relates to the eternal interests of the soul
   C. portrays a lack of character

5. The union of the faithful on earth, the   5. C
   blessed in heaven, and the souls in purgatory
   with Christ as the Head is called the
   A. Church Militant
   B. Church Triumphant
   C. Communion of Saints
   D. souls in purgatory

6. "I am the vine, you are the branches. He   6. D
   who abides in me and I in him, he bears
   much fruit; for without me you can do
   nothing." This refers particularly to
   A. actual grace
   B. sacramental grace
   C. the necessity of good works
   D. sanctifying grace

7. The first requisite for a fruitful Catholic   7. B
   life is
   A. attendance at all parish devotions
   B. personal holiness
   C. obedience to the laws of civil government
   D. reading the Bible

8. One becomes a member of Christ's Mystical   8. A
   Body by receiving
   A. Baptism   C. Holy Orders
   B. Confirmation   D. Penance

9. All members of the Church are united by   9. A
   supernatural bonds with one another and with
   Christ as their Head. This is called
   A. the Mystical Body of Christ   C. apostolic
   B. Church Triumphant   D. universal

10. "Without me you can do nothing" means   10. D
    that
    A. we should pray when we receive a sacra-
       ment
    B. we lose merit in the state of sin
    C. everything we do is pleasing to God
    D. we can do nothing to gain heaven without
       God's help

ADDITIONAL ACHIEVEMENT TESTS

PART I:

Matching Test: Match each item in Column B with an item from Column A. Print the letter of your choice in the answer blank on the right.

Column A	Column B	
1. To gain the happiness of heaven	A. The rewards Christ earned for us by His sufferings and death	A. 15
2. Apostles' Creed	B. The supernatural life of the soul	B. 9
3. Communion of Saints	C. A truth which we cannot fully understand but which we firmly believe	C. 14
4. Incarnation	D. God's loving care for us	D. 12
5. Mystical Body of Christ	E. Freedom of the Pope from error in faith and morals	E. 10
6. Indefectibility	F. We must know, love, and serve God	F. 1
7. Blessed Trinity	G. Power of the Church to teach and govern	G. 11
8. Original sin	H. The union of all the members of the Church with Christ the Head	H. 5
9. Sanctifying grace	I. The Son of God retaining His divine nature took to Himself a human nature, that is, a body and soul like ours	I. 4
10. Infallibility	J. One and the same God in Three Divine Persons	J. 7
11. Authority	K. Permanence of the Church as Christ founded it	K. 6
12. Divine Providence	L. Created spirits without bodies, having understanding and free will	L. 13
13. Angels	M. The union of the faithful on earth, the blessed in heaven, and the souls in purgatory	M. 3
14. Supernatural mystery	N. A summary of the teachings of Christ through the Catholic Church	N. 2
15. Merits	O. Inherited by all mankind except the Blessed Virgin	O. 8
16. Redemption		— 16

PART II:

Multiple Choice: Choose the correct answer for each question, and print the letter of your choice in the space on the right.

1. The special prayer in honor of the Blessed   1. C
   Trinity is the
   A. Act of Love   C. Glory Be
   B. Our Father   D. Confiteor

2. Besides knowing God by our natural reason, we can also know Him from — 2. B
   A. our prayers
   B. supernatural revelation
   C. His perfections
   D. the beatitudes

3. We find the chief truths taught by Jesus Christ in the — 3. C
   A. Commandments of the Church
   B. beatitudes
   C. Apostles' Creed
   D. Commandments of God

4. All members of the Church are united by supernatural bonds with one another and with Christ as their Head. This is called — 4. D
   A. Church Suffering
   B. Church Triumphant
   C. Church Militant
   D. the Mystical Body of Christ

5. "Preach the Gospel to all nations" indicates the Church's — 5. A
   A. universality
   B. infallibility
   C. holiness
   D. authority

6. Mary's preservation from original sin is called her — 6. A
   A. Immaculate Conception
   B. Annunciation
   C. Assumption
   D. Nativity

7. Christ said to Peter: "I will give to thee the keys to the kingdom of heaven." The keys are the symbol of — 7. C
   A. indefectibility
   B. unity
   C. authority
   D. infallibility

8. Because God made all things from nothing by His almighty power, we say that He is the — 8. B
   A. Prophet
   B. Creator
   C. Redeemer
   D. Sanctifier

9. When we say that the Pope cannot err in teaching a doctrine of faith or morals, we mean that the Pope is — 9. D
   A. one
   B. universal
   C. apostolic
   D. infallible

10. The invisible head of the Church is — 10. C
    A. pastor
    B. Sovereign Pontiff
    C. Jesus Christ
    D. bishop

11. Jesus Christ offered His sufferings and death to God as a fitting sacrifice in satisfaction for the sins of men, and regained for them the right to be the heirs of heaven. This is called the — 11. C
    A. crucifixion
    B. incarnation
    C. redemption
    D. ascension

12. The greatest happiness of heaven consists in seeing — 12. A
    A. God
    B. the Blessed Virgin
    C. the angels
    D. our parents

13. A good Catholic is one who — 13. D
    A. keeps only the Commandments of God
    B. goes to confession and Communion once a year
    C. pays his pew rent regularly
    D. believes all that the Church teaches and does all it commands

14. Catholics believe that in God there — 14. D
    A. are both three natures and three persons
    B. are three natures
    C. is one Person
    D. are three Divine Persons

15. Father, Son, and Holy Spirit are — 15. D
    A. distinct but not equal
    B. neither equal nor distinct
    C. equal but not distinct
    D. both equal and distinct

Essay Questions

1. Explain the words of our Lord: "I am the way, and the truth, and the life" (Jn. 14:6).
2. List the ways in which Christ makes use of the parish: (a) to teach; (b) to rule and guide; (c) to sanctify ourselves and others.

REFERENCES AND MATERIALS

UNIT ONE — CHRIST TEACHES US THROUGH HIS CHURCH

A. Pupil References

Anderson, Floyd, *The Bishop's Boy* (Milwaukee: Bruce, 1957).

Attwater, Donald, *A Catholic Dictionary* (New York: Macmillan, 1949).

Bedier, Julie, *My Book About God* (New York: Macmillan, 1948).

Burton, Catherine, *The Great Mantle* (New York: Longmans, 1950).

Charitas, Sister M., S.S.N.D., *Character Calendar* (Milwaukee: Bruce).

Croft, Aloysius, *Twenty-One Saints* (Milwaukee: Bruce, 1937).

Dorcy, Sr. M. Jean, *Mary, My Mother* (New York: Sheed & Ward, 1944).

Doyle, Charles Hugo, *We Have a Pope* (Paterson, N. J.: St. Anthony Press, 1942).

Greenstock, David L., *Christopher's Talks to Catholic Children* (London: Burnes, Oates, 1939).

Hunt, Marigold, *Life of Our Lord for Children* (New York: Sheed & Ward, 1939).

—— *The First Catholics* (New York: Sheed & Ward, 1954).

Johnson, G., Hannon, J.D., and Dominica, Sr. M., *Story of the Church* (New York: Benziger Bros.).

Kelly, Rev. Wm. R., Goebel, Rev. Edmund J., Imelda, Sr. Mary, and Schumacher, Rev., *Living in God's Church* (New York: Benziger Bros., 1948).

Kirsch-Brendan, *Catholic Faith*, Book Three (New York: Kenedy, 1951).

Margaret Patrice, Sr., *Keeper of the Gate* (Milwaukee: Bruce, 1941).

——— *Up the Shining Path* (Milwaukee: Bruce, 1947).

Matimore, P. H., *Heroes of God's Church* (New York: Macmillan).

Moseley, Daisy, *Sunshine and Saints* (New York: Kenedy, 1935).

Newcomb, Covelle, *Larger Than the Sky* (New York: Longmans, Green & Co., Inc., 1945).

O'Brien, Isidore, O.F.M., *The Life of Christ* (Paterson, N. J.: St. Anthony Press, 1937).

Reinhold, H. A., *Our Parish: House of God and Gate of Heaven* (New York: Paulist Press, 1943).

Thompson, Blanche J., *The Oldest Story* (Milwaukee: Bruce, 1943).

Treacy, Gerald, *Heaven's Beginning: Simplified Encyclical on the Mystical Body of Christ* (New York: Paulist Press).

——— *Stories of the Apostles for Children* (New York: Paulist Press, 1942).

Vance, Marguerite, *On Wings of Fire* (New York: E. P. Dutton & Co., Inc., 1955).

Windeatt, Mary Fabyan, *Man on Fire* (St. Paul: Grail Publications).

B. Teacher References

Aylward, Rev. Stephen, *Catechism Comes to Life* (St. Paul: Catechetical Guild, 1942).

Baierl, Joseph, *The Creed Explained* (St. Paul: Catechetical Guild, 1943).

Bandas, Rudolph, *Religion Teaching and Practice* (New York: Wagner, 1935).

Butler, Alban, *The Lives of the Saints*, revised by Donald Attwater and Herbert Thurston (New York: Kenedy, 1956), 4 vols.

Cavanaugh, Rev. W. J., *A Manual for the Teachers of Religion* (Milwaukee: Bruce, 1951).

Collins, Rev. Joseph, *Catechetical Games and Plays* (St. Paul: Catechetical Guild, 1939).

Chisholm, *The Catechism in Examples* (New York: Benziger Bros.).

Connell, Francis J., *The New Confraternity Edition, Revised, Baltimore Catechism No. 3* (New York: Benziger Bros., 1956).

Drinkwater, Rev. F. H., *More Catechism Stories* (Westminster Md.: Newman Press, 1948).

——— *Teaching the Catechism* (Westminster, Md.: Newman Press, 1953).

Fitzpatrick, Edward, and Tanner, Paul F., *Methods of Teaching Religion in Elementary Schools* (Milwaukee: Bruce, 1939).

Greenstock, David L., *Christopher's Talks to Catholic Children* (London: Burns, Oates, 1946).

Guyot, G. H., *Scriptural References for the Baltimore Catechism* (New York: Wagner, 1946).

Horan, E., *Handbook for Teachers of Religion Grades 6, 7, 8* (New York: W. H. Sadlier, Inc., 1945, 1947).

Kelly, Bernard J., *The Sacraments of Daily Life* (New York: Sheed & Ward, 1941).

Knecht, Frederick J., *Practical Commentary on Holy Scripture* (St. Louis: Herder, 1930).

Murphy, Rev. John L., *The Living Christ* (Milwaukee: Bruce, 1952).

Pius XI, *Encyclical on the Kingship of Christ* (Washington, D. C.: N.C.W.C., 1927).

Pius XII, *Encyclical on Mystical Body* (Washington, D. C.: N.C.W.C., 1955).

Prat, Ferdinand, *The Life of Christ* (Milwaukee: Bruce, 1950).

Ricciotti, Abbot Giuseppe, *The Life of Christ* (School Edition) (Milwaukee: Bruce, 1952).

Russell, William, *Christ the Leader* (Milwaukee: Bruce, 1937).

Schumacher, Msgr. M. A., *I Teach the Catechism*, Vol. III (New York: Benziger Bros., 1946).

Sheehan, Michael, *Apologetics and Catholic Doctrine* (Westminster, Md.: Newman Press, 1942).

Sloyan, Rev. G., Stulhmueller, Rev. C., et al., *New Testament Reading Guide*, 14 pamphlets (Collegeville, Minn.: Liturgical Press, 1960).

Spirago, Francis, and Clarke, Richard, *The Catechism Explained* (New York: Benziger, 1927).

Strasser, Bernard, O.S.B., *With Christ Through the Year* (Milwaukee: Bruce, 1957).

Sullivan, John T., *Externals of the Catholic Church* (New York: Kenedy).

Van Treeck, and Croft, A., rev. ed., *Symbols in the Church* (Milwaukee: Bruce, 1961).

C. Pamphlets

Betowski, *The True Church, Its Marks and Attributes* (New York: Paulist Press).

Connell, *The Power of the Holy Ghost* (New York: Paulist Press).

Forrest, M., *The Ideal Friendship* (New York: Paulist Press).

Gibbons, *Catholic Loyalty* (New York: Paulist Press).

Hurley, W., *There Is a God* (New York: Paulist Press).

Lord, Rev. D., *Gateway of Grace — Your Parish Church* (St. Louis: Queen's Work).

——— *Have You a Soul?* (St. Louis: Queen's Work).

O'Toole, J., *What Is Catholic Action?* (New York: Paulist Press).

Spense, *The Ideal Parishioner* (New York: Paulist Press).

Willmann, D., *Personality of Christ* (St. Louis: Queen's Work).

D. Materials (Audio-Visual Aids)

CHARTS:

Prayer Charts, two charts: 22 x 28 (St. Paul: Catechetical Guild).

The Test and Four Marks of the Church, CG.

The Grace of God, Sisters of the Cong. de N.D., Montreal, Canada.

FILMSTRIPS: *On the Creed:*

Life of Jesus, Catechetical Guild, Educational Society, St. Paul 2, Minn.

The Creed, St. John's University.

Catholic Pioneers and Builders of America, Eye Gate House, Inc., Jamaica, N. Y.

The Saints are Real, Eye Gate House, Inc., Jamaica, N. Y.

Heroes of the Old Testament, Eye Gate House, Inc., Jamaica, N. Y.

Rome — the Vatican, Encyclopaedia Britannica, 1150 Wilmette Ave., Wilmette, Ill.

Lourdes, Encyclopaedia Britannica, 1150 Wilmette Ave., Wilmette, Ill.

The Holy Bible in Pictures, Encyclopaedia Britannica, 1150 Wilmette Ave., Wilmette, Ill.

The Life of Christ, Society for Visual Education, Inc., Chicago, Ill.

The Roman Catholic Church Today, Society for Visual Education, Inc., Chicago, Ill.

The Apostles' Creed, Society for Visual Education, Chicago, Ill.

GAMES:

"Apostles' Creed Kwiz Game," Catechetical Guild, Educational Society, St. Paul 2, Minn.

"Creed Crown Game," Catechetical Guild, Educational Society, St. Paul 2, Minn.

PICTURES:

"Apostles' Creed," set of 65 pictures on gummed paper, Catechetical Guild.

"Apostolic Church Project Sheet," Catechetical Guild.

"Life of Christ Picture Series," Catechetical Guild.

"Life of the Church Picture Series," Catechetical Guild.

RECORDINGS:

Catholic Prayers: Creed. Record No. 1046. Natl. Cath. Recording Specialist.

SLIDES:

"Apostles' Creed," Co-op Parish.

SYMBOLS:

Apostles' Creed Symbol Set, Catechetical Guild.

Liturgical Symbols, St. John's Abbey, Collegeville, Minn.

WORKBOOKS:

"Creation Color Book," Catechetical Guild.

"Project Lessons on Apostles' Creed," Catechetical Guild.

"Story of Creation Workbook," Catechetical Guild.

UNIT TWO. THE LAWS OF LOVE ARE THE LAWS OF LIVING

(Text, pp. 47–179)

OUTLINE OF CONTENT

I. **Jesus Christ and the Commandments in General — A Review**
(Text, pp. 50–64; Baltimore Catechism, Lesson 15)

II. **Jesus Christ and the First Three Commandments — A Review**
(Text, pp. 65–85; Baltimore Catechism, Lessons 16–18)

III. **Jesus Christ and the Last Seven Commandments**
(Text, pp. 86–145; Baltimore Catechism, Lessons 19–20)

IV. **The Laws of Christ's Church**
(Text, pp. 146–173; Baltimore Catechism, Lessons 21–22)

SECTION I: Jesus Christ and the Commandments in General

(Text, pp. 50–64; Baltimore Catechism, Lesson 15)

OUTLINE OF UNIT TWO, SECTION I

A. **Faith Without Good Works Is Dead** (Text, pp. 50–52)

B. **The Law of God Is the Law of Love** (Text, pp. 52–58)
 1. The Corporal Works of Mercy Relieve the Physical Needs of Our Neighbor's Body (Text, pp. 53–54)
 2. The Spiritual Works of Mercy Relieve the Spiritual Needs of Our Neighbor's Soul (Text, pp. 54–57)
 3. The Works of Mercy Are an Obligation (Text, pp. 57–58)

C. **Christ Invites Man to the Life of Perfection** (Text, pp. 59–60)

TEACHING SUGGESTIONS FOR UNIT TWO, SECTION I

I. OBJECTIVES

A. Primary Objective

To realize that God's laws are guideposts He has given us to help us win happiness, both on earth and forever in heaven.

B. Auxiliary Objectives

For the Intellect:

1. To increase our knowledge of the laws of God and His Church.
2. To understand that the Commandments are the expression of God's will for us.

For the Will:

1. To observe the Commandments of God and the Church as a manifestation of our love of God.
2. To bestow material and spiritual help on those in need.

II. NOTES ON TEACHER PRESENTATION

A. Suggestions for Developing Understanding of Subject Matter

1. Read and discuss the story of the two great Commandments as told by St. Matthew 22:34–40.
2. Present filmstrip on the Commandments.
3. Discuss how laws in general help us.
4. Show by comparison with certain civil laws that the laws of God are given to us for our happiness and well-being.
5. Bring out the idea that only by keeping God's law can we expect to enjoy any measure of peace and happiness.
6. Direct attention to the order and beauty of nature brought about by the observance of God's plan.
7. Recall some of the works of mercy practiced by our Lord.
8. Tell of occasions on which you have observed persons perform works of mercy.

B. Correlating Activities

1. Read these scriptural references to the Commandments:
 a) Mt. 19:17
 b) Jn. 14:15
 c) Jn. 15:10
 d) Lk. 1:6

2. Use one of the scriptural references on the Commandments as an art lettering project.
3. Read the account of God giving the Commandments to Moses (Exod. 20:1–17).
4. Conduct a panel discussion on the necessity of the Commandments.
5. Discuss a sport in which children are intensely interested. Show how rules are a necessity for the success and enjoyment of the game. Challenge children to think of some game that is played without rules.
6. Study catechism material referring to the Commandments in general.
7. Read and discuss the story of the Good Samaritan (Lk. 10:25–37).
8. Gather stories and pictures from mission magazines illustrating the performance of the works of mercy.

C. Application

1. Be grateful to God for giving us these guides in helping us get to heaven.
2. Co-operate with the grace of God in the observance of His law, especially when such observance is difficult.
3. Be ready to do good deeds even when they are not required.

III. EVALUATION

PART I: Completion. Supply the missing word or words. Place your answer in the column at the right.

1. The Ten Commandments were given by God Himself to (1) on (2) and (3) confirmed them.
2. Another name for the Ten Commandments is (4).
3. Deeds to help others in body and soul when done in the name of Christ are called (5).
4. The laws of God bind (6).
5. In order to be saved one must belong to the (7) and he must also keep the (8) of God and of the (9).

1. Moses
2. Mt. Sinai
3. Christ our Lord
4. Decalogue
5. works of mercy
6. all men
7. Church
8. Commandments
9. Church

PART II: What work of mercy is performed in each of the following cases?

1. Agnes warns her friend Mary about a dangerous occasion of sin.
2. Joe visits a classmate who is recovering from a siege of polio.
3. A group of neighboring children stop in to comfort a friend whose mother is seriously ill.
4. A group of eighth grade children offer the rosary for a deceased father of one of their classmates.
5. During a parish clothes drive for the needy Mary gives up a dress of which she is especially fond.

1. spiritual
2. corporal
3. corporal
4. spiritual
5. corporal

IV. ANSWERS TO STUDY EXERCISES FOR UNIT TWO, SECTION I

(Text, pp. 61–62)

I. Multiple Choice (p. 61):

1. D	4. C	7. B
2. A	5. B	8. D
3. A	6. C	9. A

II. Problems for Discussion (p. 61):
Answers will vary.

SECTION II: Jesus Christ and the First Three Commandments — A Review

(Text, pp. 65–85; Baltimore Catechism, Lessons, 16–18)

OUTLINE OF UNIT TWO, SECTION II

A. The First Commandment of God Is: "I Am the Lord Thy God; Thou Shalt Not Have Strange Gods Before Me" (Text, pp. 65–69)
   1. We Worship God by Faith (Text, pp. 66–67)
   2. We Worship God by Hope (Text, p. 68)
   3. We Worship God by Charity (Text, pp. 68–69)

B. The Second Commandment of God Is: "Thou Shalt Not Take the Name of the Lord Thy God in Vain" (Text, pp. 70–72)

C. The Third Commandment of God Is: "Remember Thou Keep Holy the Lord's Day" (Text, pp. 72–74)
   1. Keep Holy the Lord's Day (pp. 73–74)
   2. Avoid Servile Work (p. 74)

TEACHING SUGGESTIONS FOR UNIT TWO, SECTION II

I. OBJECTIVES

A. Primary Objective

To realize the significance of these three Commandments as means for showing us how we are to act with respect to our Lord and Creator.

B. Auxiliary Objectives

For the Intellect:

1. To review the three Commandments which have to do with our relationship to Almighty God.
2. To acquire sufficient knowledge of the value of faith that we really live it.

For the Will:

1. To observe faithfully these Commandments in recognition of God as our Lord and Creator.
2. To develop an intense desire to show honor and respect for God's name.
3. To guard our holy Faith as our most cherished possession.
4. To be faithful in attending Mass on all days of obligation.

II. NOTES ON TEACHER PRESENTATION

A. Suggestions for Developing Understanding of Subject Matter

1. Recall that this material on the first three Commandments is review work.
2. Have children give examples of "false gods" of our day.
3. Discuss the life of one's patron saint, bringing out the particular virtue for which that saint was noted.
4. Discuss means that can be employed to help ourselves and others show reverence for God's name.
5. Your neighborhood friend attends the Protestant church at the corner of your street. One day he asks you to attend services at his church on Sunday and promises that he will attend the Catholic church with you the following Sunday. Would you be free to go with him? How would you explain this matter to him?
6. Joe always carries a small brass charm for good luck. You point out how foolish he is, but he points to the scapular medal you are wearing around your neck and tells you that you are just as foolish as he is. How will you explain the difference to Joe?
7. What would you do to help a boy overcome the bad habit of using God's name in vain?
8. While playing in your schoolyard you hear a small child in a nearby group use God's name in a fit of temper. Some of the older boys laugh and think it extremely funny. What would you say to those boys? What would you do to help that youngster?
9. A salesman is on the way to a small town to attend Sunday Mass. Along the way he meets an elderly couple having serious car trouble. He stops and gives them some assistance even though he knows that he might miss Mass. Would he be justified in doing that?

B. Correlating Activities

1. Make a list of common superstitious practices which children may have observed.
2. Discuss some of the activities carried on by the Holy Name Society in the parish.
3. Make a visit to the parish church and neighboring churches to note what statues and images of saints are found there.
4. Read and discuss — Acts 3:1-10
5. Make plans for assisting someone who finds it difficult to get to Mass on Sunday.
6. Arrange a bulletin board on pictures of our patron saints.

C. Application

1. Recite the Divine Praises reverently in reparation for disrespect to God's holy name.
2. Be sensible in devotion to the saints.
3. Ask your own patron saint for help in imitating his virtues.

III. EVALUATION

MULTIPLE CHOICE: Choose the correct answer and print the letter of your choice in the space on the right.

1. Belief that all religions are equal is known as   1. B
   A. heresy   B. indifferentism   C. schism

2. A false oath is known as   2. B
   A. calumny   B. perjury   C. slander

3. To use God's name in common talk is ordinarily a   3. C
   A. mortal sin   B. sacrilege   C. venial sin

4. By keeping the First Commandment of God we   4. B
   A. show respect for God's name
   B. acknowledge God as our Supreme Lord and Master
   C. offer sacrifice to His name

5. A person who believes that he can be saved without the help of God commits the sin of   5. B
   A. blasphemy
   B. presumption
   C. superstition

6. A Catholic who takes part in non-Catholic worship commits a sin against   6. C
   A. justice   B. charity   C. faith

7. The calling down of some evil on a person, place, or thing is   7. C
   A. swearing   B. blasphemy   C. cursing

8. A baptized person who completely rejects the truths of the Catholic Faith is   8. A
   A. an apostate   B. a heretic   C. an infidel

9. We should avoid profanity   9. C
   A. to control our tongues
   B. because such language advertises our ignorance
   C. to show respect for God's holy name

10. On the first tablet of stone are Commandments which indicate our duties to   10. A
    A. God   B. neighbor   C. ourselves

IV. ANSWERS TO STUDY EXERCISES FOR UNIT TWO, SECTION II

(Text, pp. 75–76)

I. Yes or No:

1. Yes	5. Yes	9. Yes
2. Yes	6. No	10. Yes
3. No	7. Yes	11. Yes
4. Yes	8. Yes	12. No

II. Matching:

1. H	3. E	5. A	7. G	9. F
2. B	4. J	6. D	8. I	10. C

SECTION III: Jesus Christ and the Last Seven Commandments

(Text, pp. 86–145; Baltimore Catechism, Lessons 19–20)

OUTLINE OF UNIT TWO, SECTION III

A. The Fourth Commandment of God Is: "Honor Thy Father and Thy Mother" (Text, pp. 86–93)

1. Obedience and Respect Are Due to Parents (Text, pp. 86-88)
2. Respect and Obedience Are Due to All Lawful Superiors (Text, pp. 88–89)
3. Good Catholics Are Good Citizens (Text, pp. 90–92)

B. The Fifth Commandment of God Is: "Thou Shalt Not Kill" (Text, pp. 95–114)

1. Jesus Christ Teaches Us How to Observe This Commandment (Text, pp. 96–97)
2. Care of Our Physical and Spiritual Welfare Is Required (Text, pp. 97–100)
3. Sins Forbidden by the Fifth Commandment (Text, pp. 100–111)

C. The Sixth Commandment of God Is: "Thou Shalt Not Commit Adultery" (Text, pp. 114–119)

The Ninth Commandment of God Is: "Thou Shalt Not Covet Thy Neighbor's Wife" (Text, pp. 120–124)

THE SIXTH COMMANDMENT OF GOD

1. Impurity and Immodesty Are Forbidden (Text, pp. 115–118)
2. How Chastity Can Be Preserved (Text, pp. 118–119)

THE NINTH COMMANDMENT OF GOD

1. Willful Thoughts About Impure Things Are Sinful (Text, pp. 120)
2. Thoughts About Impure Things Are Not Always Sinful (Text, pp. 120–121)
3. Bad Thoughts Are Sinful If Deliberate (Text, p. 121)

D. The Seventh Commandment of God Is: "Thou Shalt Not Steal" (Text, pp. 124–131)

The Tenth Commandment of God Is: "Thou Shalt Not Covet Thy Neighbor's Goods" (Text, pp. 131–132)

THE SEVENTH COMMANDMENT

1. Respect What Belongs to Others (Text, pp. 125–126)
2. Live Up to Business Agreements (Text, p. 126)
3. Pay Just Debts (Text, pp. 127–128)
4. Dishonesty Is Forbidden (Text, pp. 128–131)

E. The Eighth Commandment of God Is: "Thou Shalt Not Bear False Witness Against Thy Neighbor" (Text, pp. 134–145)

1. Christ Teaches by Word and Example the Virtue of Truthfulness (Text, p. 135)
2. We Are to Be Truthful in Speech (Text, pp. 136–142)

    a) Lies (pp. 136–139)
    b) Rash Judgment (p. 139)
    c) Detraction (pp. 139–140)
    d) Keeping Secrets Is an Obligation (pp. 140–142)

3. Charity Covers a Multitude of Sins (Text, pp. 142–143)

TEACHING SUGGESTIONS FOR UNIT TWO, SECTION III

I. OBJECTIVES

A. Primary Objective

To realize the significance of these last seven Commandments as a means of showing us how to love God through love for our neighbor and ourself.

B. Auxiliary Objectives

For the Intellect:

1. To understand the necessity of showing our love for God by love for our fellow men.
2. To learn how each one of these Commandments can be observed in daily life.
3. To realize that God reveals His will for us in each Commandment.
4. To learn what each Commandment requires and what it forbids.
5. To develop the ability to distinguish between temptation and sin.
6. To realize that interest in the well-being of others must be universal.
7. To understand the need of laws governing the social life of man.

For the Will:

1. To practice the virtues of justice and charity in dealing with our fellow men.
2. To emphasize kindness especially to those of other nations and races.
3. To obey all lawful authority because it comes from God.
4. To be peace-loving in all our dealings with our neighbor.
5. To practice purity and modesty in all thought and outward behavior.
6. To respect all property rights of others.
7. To develop the habit of being satisfied with what we have and in sharing what we have with others.
8. To think well of others and put a favorable construction on their actions.
9. To be fair and honest in all that we have to do with others.

II. NOTES ON TEACHER PRESENTATION

A. Suggestions for Developing Understanding of Subject Matter

1. Read and discuss the finding of Jesus in the Temple. What did Christ wish to teach us in this incident?

2. How did our Lord stress the fact that we must render obedience to civil authority? Can you mention examples where He Himself rendered such obedience?
3. Explain how parents share in the authority of God.
4. Tell the story of Absalom's unfaithfulness to his father David and his final punishment.
5. How often do you pray for the successful handling of problems that concern the welfare of the country? the world?
6. List and discuss local civil affairs in which children may participate.
7. Make suggestions for helping boys and girls who tend to be quarrelsome.
8. Show how traffic rules help eliminate dangers to life.
9. Read and discuss Commander Shea's last letter to his son Jackie.
10. From your observations around the school and on the playground could you call attention to things that should be checked or discontinued if children are to observe the Fifth Commandment?
11. Prepare a three-minute talk on the necessity of the Fifth Commandment if we are to live as reasonable beings who respect the dignity of our fellow men.
12. Explain why the Church condemns company-keeping and excessive dating by elementary school children.
13. Show how being content with what we have and sharing with others can be a positive means of observing the Seventh and Tenth Commandments.
14. Relate any personal experience you may have had to prove that "honesty is the best policy."
15. How did our Lord feel about the reputation of others? Can you give examples to prove your point?
16. Discuss what means can be used to help one another develop a love of truth.
17. What does St. Matthew have to say about lies (Mt. 26:59–61)?
18. Read Proverbs 6:16–19. What does it say of talebearing?

B. Correlating Activities
1. Make a list of all the ways you can show love and respect for your parents.
2. Show by your conduct that you have reverence for authority because it comes from God.
3. Reproduce and explain the symbols of the Commandments that refer to our neighbor.
4. Prove by giving examples that the spirit of forgiveness helps safeguard life and promotes peace in a community.
5. Tell the story of the unmerciful servant from St. Matthew 18:21–35.
6. Write a composition on "The Power of Good Example."

7. Every week check the Legion of Decency ratings for the pictures being shown in your local theaters.
8. Conduct a panel discussion: "Commandments Are Guides to Real Happiness."
9. List ways in which restitution can be made.
10. Scan a newspaper for possible violations of the Commandments.
11. Read and tell to which Commandment reference is being made:

Mk. 9:41	Mk. 9:41–47
Mt. 17:23–26	Prov. 26:18–19
Acts 5:1–10	Mt. 12:1–14
Prov. 22:1	Rom. 13:1–18
Mk. 10:23–27	Mt. 28:18–20
Lk. 12:13–21	Mt. 25:14–30
Num. 35:16–21	

12. Make a chart indicating what is commanded and what is forbidden by each Commandment.

How would you solve these problems?
1. Tom went to the store for his mother and by making a purchase at a sale price was able to save twenty-five cents. He felt that because he saved that much he was entitled to spend it without asking his mother. What do you think?
2. Helen is anxious to see a movie at a local theater but will not check the list to see whether or not it is permitted. She goes and then, upon consulting the list, finds it is forbidden. She claims she has done no wrong. Has she?
3. If you saw a child damaging school property in some way, would you do anything about it or would you just pass it by as being "none of your business"?
4. A boy in your room has been found guilty of stealing. Weeks later you miss some money from your coat pocket. Would you be justified in thinking or saying that he is again guilty of stealing?
5. Bill's mother tells him she does not wish him to keep company with certain companions who are of questionable reputation. Bill insists they are all right and that his mother is just being old fashioned about the whole matter. What would you say to Bill?

C. Application
1. Be obedient to all lawful authority.
2. Think kindly; speak kindly.
3. Refuse to listen to gossip.
4. Cultivate a spirit of generosity.
5. Be modest: in dress, in word, in looks, in actions.
6. Avoid those companions who may be an occasion of sin.
7. Rejoice with companions who may have succeeded in some particular project.
8. Be honest and truthful in all your dealings and help others to do the same.
9. Help maintain peace at home, at school, and on the playground.

10. Always be a source of good example — especially to younger children and those not of our faith.

III. EVALUATION

Identification: Write your answer in front of the statement.

PART I: Which Commandment is violated in each of the following:

9 th	1.	Harvey does not try to banish impure thoughts which come into his mind.
10 th	2.	Albert desires to take Vincent's ball and will if he gets the chance.
1 st	3.	Tim carries a charm in his pocket to keep him from harm.
2 nd	4.	Rose frequently uses the word "God" when there is no good reason for doing so.
8 th	5.	Margaret says that her schoolmate, Virginia, is dishonest in school, but she knows that her story is not true.
1 st	6.	Eileen neglects to learn Christian Doctrine.
6 th	7.	Harry reads an indecent magazine.
5 th	8.	Bill and Bob meet after school in order to settle an argument by means of a fight.
7 th	9.	Irene borrows some money from her friend, but she does not intend to repay it.
1 st	10.	Fred expects to be saved, but he does not pray or receive the Sacraments.
5 th	11.	Helen becomes quite angry on account of the actions of her baby sister.
3 rd	12.	Mary sews on Sunday just to pass away the time.
4 th	13.	Edward refuses to obey his teacher in school.
7 th	14.	Cheating.
3 rd	15.	Stealing from another person.
7 th	16.	Never praying.
1 st	17.	Telling a lie.
8 th	18.	Missing Mass on Sunday through my own fault.
2 nd	19.	Using God's name carelessly.
4 th	20.	Disobeying.
5 th	21.	Murder.
5 th	22.	Anger.
5 th	23.	Suicide.
9 th	24.	Impure thoughts.
6 th	25.	Impure acts.
7 th	26.	Damaging property.
8 th	27.	Telling secrets.

PART II: Do the same with the following exercise — show which Commandment is being observed in each of the following:

8 th	1.	John tells the truth even though he knows his father will punish him.
8 th	2.	Whenever anyone says anything unkind about other people Joan always says something good.
4 th	3.	Jane comes promptly when her mother calls her.

6 th	4.	Helen imitates the Blessed Virgin in her personal life.
9 th	5.	Jack says ejaculations when tempted to impure thoughts.

IV. ANSWERS TO STUDY EXERCISES FOR UNIT TWO, SECTION III

(Text, pp. 92–93, 112–113, 122–123, 132–133, 143–144)

A. The Fourth Commandment (pp. 92–93)

I. Completion (p. 92):
1. that is not sinful
2. God
3. voting honestly and without selfish motives; paying just taxes; defending his country's rights when necessary

II. Multiple Choice (p. 93):
1. B   2. B

III. Yes or No (p. 93):
1. No   2. Yes   3. No   4. No   5. No

IV. Questions for Discussion (p. 93):
Answers will vary.

B. The Fifth Commandment (pp. 112–113)

I. Matching (p. 112):
1. C   3. F   5. A
2. E   4. B   6. D

II. Completion (p. 112):
1. suicide   3. anger   5. hatred   7. revenge
2. murder   4. life   6. scandal

III. True or False (p. 113)
1. True   3. False   5. True   7. False
2. True   4. True   6. True   8. True

C. Sixth and Ninth Commandments (p. 122)

Matching (p. 122):
1. C   3. B   5. F   7. I   9. G
2. A   4. E   6. D   8. J   10. H

D. Seventh and Tenth Commandments (pp. 132–133)

Yes or No (pp. 132–133):
1. No   3. Yes   5. Yes   7. Yes   9. Yes
2. Yes   4. No   6. No   8. Yes   10. Yes

E. Eighth Commandment (p. 143)

Matching (p. 143):
1. C   2. D   3. B   4. A

SECTION IV: The Laws of Christ's Church

(Text, pp. 146–178; Baltimore Catechism, Lessons 21–22)

OUTLINE OF UNIT II, SECTION IV

A. The First Commandment of the Church Is: "To Assist at Mass on All Sundays and Holydays of Obligation" (Text, pp. 148—151)

B. The Second Commandment of the Church Is: "To Fast and Abstain on the Days Appointed" (Text, pp. 151—155)

   1. Certain Days Are Set Aside as Fast Days (Text, p. 154)

   2. All Fridays of the Year and Certain Other Days Are Days of Abstinence (Text, pp. 154—155)

C. The Third Commandment of the Church Is: "To Confess Our Sins at Least Once a Year"
The Fourth Commandment of the Church Is: "To Receive the Holy Eucharist During the Easter Time" (Text, pp. 155—158)

   1. We Are Strictly Obliged to Make a Good Confession at Least Once a Year If We Are in Mortal Sin (Text, pp. 156—157)

   2. To Neglect to Receive Holy Communion During the Easter Time Is a Mortal Sin (Text, pp. 157—158)

D. The Fifth Commandment of the Church Is: "To Contribute to the Support of the Church" (Text, 159—161)

   1. The Faithful Must Share in the Support of the Holy See (Text, p. 160)

   2. The Faithful Must Share in the Support of the Diocese (Text, p. 160)

   3. The Faithful Must Share in the Support of the Parish (Text, pp. 160—161)

E. The Sixth Commandment of the Church Is: "To Observe the Laws of the Church Concerning Marriage" (Text, pp. 162—165)

   1. It Is Forbidden to Contract Marriage With Non-Catholics (Text, pp. 163—164)

   2. Marriage With a Second Cousin or Any Relative Closer Than a Second Cousin Is Forbidden (Text, p. 164)

   3. Marriage May Not Be Solemnized at Certain Times (Text, p. 165)

   4. The Ideal of the Church Is a Catholic Marriage at a Nuptial Mass (Text, p. 165)

TEACHING SUGGESTIONS FOR UNIT TWO, SECTION IV

I. OBJECTIVES

A. Primary Objective

To develop a better understanding of our duties and responsibilities as members of Christ's Church, and to appreciate the interest of the Church in our salvation.

B. Auxiliary Objectives

For the Intellect:

1. To increase our knowledge of the laws of the Church.
2. To know that these laws are human laws and can be changed or dispensed with by the same authority.
3. To learn our duty of contributing to the support of the Church.
4. To understand our obligation to fast and abstain on days appointed.
5. To realize that our contributing to the Church is a matter of justice and not charity.

For the Will:

1. To accept willingly any changes made by the Church in her precepts.
2. To resolve never to miss Mass on Sunday or any other day of obligation.
3. To train ourselves in the practice of voluntary self-denial.

II. NOTES ON TEACHER PRESENTATION

A. Suggestions for Developing Understanding of Subject Matter

1. Bulletin-board display picturing Christ, the Holy Father, the Bishop, and the pastor; illustrations depicting precepts of the Church.
2. Discuss the fact that by Baptism we become members of the Church. As such we assume the responsibility of obeying her laws.
3. Compare rules and regulations made in a family, club, or some society with the laws of the Church. Discuss the value and necessity of rules in any well-organized society.
4. Discuss the importance of public worship on the part of members of the Church.
5. Show by specific example that as members of the same Church we have obligations to help one another.
6. Explain the difference between fast and abstinence.
7. Read the account of how Christ gave us the example of fasting.
8. Recall how the early Christians offered Mass in the Catacombs. Why?
9. Why do children abstain but not fast?
10. Report on some of the recent changes in the laws of the Church.
11. Consider the necessity of penance as a means of reparation for sin.
12. Tell how the law of the Church concerning marriage is a safeguard of family life and happiness.
13. Give evidence that by contributing to the support of the Church you are helping to spread the word of God.
14. Read orally what Christ says about penance in St. Matthew 16:24.
15. Suggest some possible things that children could do in place of fasting.
16. Retell the stories of the institution of the Sacraments of Penance and Holy Eucharist.

B. Correlating Activities

1. Offer help to parents who find it difficult to get to Mass on days of obligation because of circumstances.
2. Make a calendar with special markings for all holydays of obligation. Assign a committee to check on those most commonly observed.
3. List from your diocesan paper special projects that are made possible by the contributions of the faithful.
4. Consult the parish priest in order to get some idea of the major expenses connected with the operation of a parish.
5. Look up and report on the lives of the saints who were outstanding for their fasting and penance.
6. Make a comparison of what you spend for recreation with what you ordinarily contribute to the Church.
7. Do what you can to help a friend or relative of yours, especially one not of the Faith, to understand some of the regulations of the Church.
8. Hold an open discussion on the obligation of using all parish property with care.
9. Investigate the reason why different holydays of obligation are observed in different countries.
10. Make a booklet of the holydays of obligation, with a short report on each holyday.
11. Write a short composition on our reasons for fast and abstinence.
12. Suggest means of encouraging frequent Holy Communion among your classmates.
13. Plan with your classmates to pray every day for those who find it difficult to conform to the laws of the Church.

C. Application

1. Offer a prayer of thanks for being a member of the Church.
2. Resolve to be faithful in assisting at Mass on all Sundays and holydays of obligation.
3. Always be prompt and show others good example of reverent participation at Mass.
4. Have a spirit of obedience for all Church regulations.
5. Be determined to receive Penance and Holy Communion frequently.
6. Practice voluntary acts of mortification.
7. Put some part of your spending money in the poor box.
8. Avoid worldly pleasures during Lent and Advent and make an offering to some mission project.
9. Show your respect and reverence for all priests.

III. EVALUATION

MULTIPLE CHOICE: Select the one word or expression that completes the sentence correctly and write the number of the answer in the space on the right.

1. Catholics do not eat meat on Friday because   1. B
   A. the Apostles were fishermen
   B. Christ died on that day
   C. they wish to be different from others
   D. too much meat is not healthful

2. Days of abstinence are those on which we   2. A
   are forbidden to eat
   A. flesh meat
   B. three full meals
   C. butter, eggs, milk, and cheese

3. I must hear Mass on   3. D
   A. Ash Wednesday
   B. Holy Thursday
   C. the feast of the Annunciation
   D. the feast of the Assumption

4. A permission officially given, which excuses   4. A
   one from keeping the law, is called
   A. a dispensation   C. a contract
   B. abstinence   D. restitution

5. The number of holydays of obligation in the   5. D
   United States is
   A. five   B. seven   C. four   D. six

6. Holydays of obligation were instituted by   6. B
   A. Christ   B. the Church   C. the Apostles

7. A Catholic who freely neglects his Easter   7. C
   duty commits
   A. no sin   C. a mortal sin
   B. a sacrilege   D. a venial sin

8. The Church commands us to worship God   8. A
   on Sunday by
   A. assisting at Mass
   B. praying the family rosary
   C. not doing any servile work
   D. performing deeds of charity

9. The best motive for assisting at Mass on   9. D
   Sunday is that
   A. it can be offered for the living and dead
   B. it is a means of gaining grace
   C. the Church commands it under pain of mortal sin
   D. it gives God the greatest honor and adoration

10. Easter time in the United States extends   10. B
    from the first Sunday of Lent to
    A. Holy Saturday
    B. Trinity Sunday
    C. Ascension
    D. Pentecost

Write the holydays of obligation.
Write the precepts of the Church.

Problem-Solving:

1. You and a Protestant friend are enjoying a Friday afternoon ball game at the Stadium. During a short

intermission he goes to the refreshment stand and brings back two hot dogs. He offers you one and when you refuse he exclaims impatiently, "I can't understand why you Catholics make such a fuss about eating meat on Friday." How would you solve this problem for him?

2. Your sister is making preparations to be married within a few months. A neighbor suggests that she have it done by a justice of the peace. She thinks this would eliminate a long wait, much preparation, and considerable expense. What would be your answer?

3. One Sunday on your way to Mass you stop to chat for a moment with your neighbor friend. She notices your collection envelope and asks you what that is. Explain the matter to her.

ACHIEVEMENT TEST

THE COMMANDMENTS OF GOD AND THE CHURCH

PART I: Multiple Choice. Underline the correct answer and print the letter of your choice in the answer space on the right.

1. A person who deliberately calls upon God to witness an untruth commits the sin of   1. A
A. perjury   C. pride
B. despair   D. blasphemy

2. If my speech or actions serve as an occasion of sin for another, I am guilty of   2. D
A. injustice   C. frankness
B. swearing   D. scandal

3. The first three Commandments indicate our duties toward   3. C
A. ourselves   C. God
B. our neighbor   D. nature

4. Only one full meal is allowed on   4. A
A. fast days   C. All Souls' Day
B. abstinence days   D. holydays

5. Taking God's name in vain is   5. C
A. cursing   C. profanity
B. blasphemy   D. calumny

6. When a person reveals the hidden faults of another without a good reason, he commits the sin of   6. A
A. detraction   C. rash judgment
B. sloth   D. scandal

7. The Ten Commandments, a code of human conduct, are also called   7. D
A. creed   C. counsels
B. precepts   D. decalogue

8. To encourage men to reverence God's name, the Church has organized the   8. D
A. Altar and Rosary Society
B. Young People's Club
C. Mission Band
D. Holy Name Society

9. The Law of God is the law of   9. D
A. mercy   C. fear
B. patience   D. love

10. The Third Commandment regulates our   10. A
A. external worship
B. speech
C. respect for our neighbor
D. obedience

11. To give back what one has taken from another unjustly is   11. C
A. robbery   C. restitution
B. stealing   D. resignation

12. The Eighth Commandment tells us to   12. C
A. lie if we can save someone
B. talk about the faults of others
C. speak the truth in all things
D. listen to gossip

13. God's Law is expressed in the   13. C
A. beatitudes
B. counsels
C. Ten Commandments
D. Commandments of the Church

14. On the first tablet of stone are Commandments which indicate our duties to   14. C
A. neighbor   C. God
B. nature   D. ourselves

15. The laws of God bind   15. B
A. only those who fear hell
B. all men
C. only Catholics
D. Jews and Catholics

16. By keeping the First Commandment of God we   16. B
A. show respect for God's Name
B. acknowledge God as our Supreme Lord and Master and offer Him adoration
C. offer sacrifice to His name
D. appreciate what He does for us

17. A boy who believes that he can be saved without the help of God commits the sin of   17. B
A. blasphemy   C. superstition
B. presumption   D. indifferentism

18. One who takes part in non-Catholic church service commits a sin against   18. D
A. justice   C. hope
B. charity   D. faith

19. A person sins by superstition when he   19. C
A. calls on God to witness a lie
B. trusts that he can be saved by his own efforts
C. attributes to a creature a power that belongs to God alone
D. believes in a false religion

20. We should avoid profanity and blasphemy 20. B
in order
   A. to control our tongues
   B. to show respect for God's holy name
   C. because such language shows a lack of
   self-respect
   D. because such language advertises our
   ignorance

21. The calling down of some evil on a person, 21. C
place, or thing is
   A. swearing   C. cursing
   B. perjury   D. blasphemy

22. A baptized person who completely rejects the 22. B
truths of the Catholic Faith is
   A. a heretic   C. a blasphemer
   B. an apostate   D. an infidel

23. The Church commands us to worship God 23. A
on Sunday by
   A. assisting at Mass
   B. praying the family rosary
   C. performing deeds of charity

24. The *best* motive for assisting at Mass on 24. D
Sundays is that
   A. it can be offered for the living and dead
   B. it is a means of gaining graces
   C. the Church commands it under pain of
   mortal sin
   D. it gives God the greatest honor and
   adoration

25. The most important thing the Fourth Com- 25. B
mandment tells us to do is to
   A. respect civil authority
   B. respect, love, and obey our parents
   C. be kind to our parents
   D. be a good citizen

26. In addition to obeying our parents we are 26. B
obliged to obey lawful superiors because
   A. they are older than we are
   B. they have authority from God
   C. we like them
   D. we will be punished if we do not obey
   them

27. "Render to Caesar the things that are Cae- 27. A
sar's," teaches us
   A. to obey the civil law
   B. to care for the sick and needy
   C. to contribute to the support of the
   Church
   D. to obey our parents

28. To be a good citizen I must 28. D
   A. safeguard my life and health
   B. respect my neighbor's good name
   C. safeguard my rights as an individual
   D. respect all civil authority and observe the
   laws of the country

29. A desire to injure others because they have 29. D
injured us is
   A. anger   C. hatred
   B. envy   D. revenge

30. The best means of preserving purity and 30. C
strengthening ourselves against temptation
is to
   A. read books on purity
   B. avoid bad companions
   C. go to confession frequently and receive
   Holy Communion as often as possible
   D. listen to the advice of parents

31. By the Sixth Commandment we are com- 31. C
manded to
   A. practice charity
   B. speak the truth at all times
   C. be modest in our outward behavior
   D. take proper care of our physical welfare

32. The Church made Friday a day of absti- 32. C
nence to remind us of Christ's
   A. resurrection   C. death on the cross
   B. ascension   D. public life

33. A Catholic who freely neglects his Easter 33. C
duty commits
   A. no sin   C. a mortal sin
   B. a sacrilege   D. a venial sin

34. The number of holydays in the United States 34. D
is
   A. five   B. seven   C. four   D. six

35. Holydays of obligation were instituted by 35. B
   A. Christ   B. the Church   C. the Apostles

36. A permission, officially given, which excuses 36. A
one from keeping the law is called
   A. a dispensation   C. a contract
   B. abstinence   D. restitution

37. The Church 37. A
   A. forbids mixed marriages
   B. is indifferent to marriages
   C. approves of mixed marriages
   D. encourages mixed marriages to insure
   better understanding among Catholics

38. The Church 38. C
   A. does not allow Catholics to marry during
   Lent
   B. forbids marriage during Advent
   C. allows Catholics to marry during Lent
   provided the marriage is not solemnized
   D. has no regulations concerning times for
   marrying

39. Days of complete abstinence are those on 39. D
which we are forbidden to eat
   A. fish   C. three full meals
   B. food between meals D. meat

33

40. Easter time in the United States is from 40. C
   A. the second Sunday of Lent to Pentecost Sunday
   B. Ash Wednesday to Holy Saturday
   C. the first Sunday of Lent to Trinity Sunday
   D. Holy Saturday to Low Sunday

41. Under pain of mortal sin we are bound to 41. D
assist at Mass on
   A. the feast of the Annunciation
   B. All Souls' Day
   C. feast of the Presentation
   D. Ascension Thursday

42. The Church forbids mixed marriages chiefly 42. A
because
   A. they are often the source of spiritual dangers
   B. they are not a fruitful source of vocations
   C. they often lead to family discord
   D. they give the children improper training

43. A Catholic who goes to a justice of the 43. A
peace or a minister to be married to a non-Catholic is
   A. not married at all and commits a grievous sin
   B. married and commits no sin
   C. really married although he commits a mortal sin
   D. not married at all and commits a venial sin

44. The marriage bond can be broken by 44. B
   A. a civil divorce
   B. the death of either party
   C. the private agreement of husband and wife
   D. the permission of the Church to live separately

IV. ANSWERS TO STUDY EXERCISES FOR UNIT TWO, SECTION IV
(Text, pp. 168–169)

I. Completion (p. 168):
1. mortal
2. (a) Christmas, Dec. 25; (b) Octave of the Nativity of Our Lord, Jan. 1: (c) Ascension, 40 days after Easter; (d) Assumption, Aug. 15; (e) All Saints, Nov. 1; (f) Immaculate Conception, Dec. 8
3. (a) fast; (b) abstinence
4. (a) First Sunday of Lent; (b) Trinity Sunday
5. Nuptial

II. Matching (p. 168):
1. B   2. D   3. C   4. E   5. A

ANSWERS TO THE ACHIEVEMENT TEST FOR UNIT TWO
(Text, pp. 174–177)

I. Multiple Choice (Text, pp. 174–176):

1. D	6. C	11. C	16. B	21. A
2. A	7. A	12. B	17. A	22. C
3. C	8. D	13. B	18. A	23. B
4. C	9. B	14. A	19. D	24. C
5. D	10. A	15. D	20. A	25. D

II. True-False (Text, pp. 176–177):

1. True	6. False	11. True	16. True
2. True	7. False	12. False	17. False
3. True	8. True	13. True	18. True
4. True	9. True	14. True	19. True
5. True	10. False	15. True	

III. Matching (Text, p. 177):

1. J	3. F	5. A	7. D	9. I
2. E	4. G	6. B	8. C	10. H

IV. Multiple Choice (Text, p. 178)

1. D	3. C	5. B	7. B	9. D
2. B	4. B	6. A	8. A	10. B

REFERENCES AND MATERIALS
UNIT TWO — THE LAWS OF LOVE ARE THE LAWS OF LIVING

A. Pupil References

Brennan, Gerald, *Toby's Shadow* (St. Paul, Minn.: Catechetical Guild).

Catholic Treasury Books (Milwaukee: Bruce).

Cornelius, Sister M., *Fifteen Saints for Girls* (Milwaukee: Bruce, 1951).

Coyne, Anne, *A Shepherd and a King, St. John Vianney* (Milwaukee: Bruce, 1939).

Dorcy, Sr. Mary Jean, O.P., *Mary, My Mother* (New York: Sheed & Ward, 1944).

Doty, Rev. Wm., *Catechetical Stories for Children* (New York: Wagner, 1948).

Farjlan, E., *Ten Saints* (New York: Oxford University Press, 1936).

Greenstock, David L., *Christopher Talks to Children*, two volumes (London: Burns, Oates, 1946).

Husslein, J. C., *Heroines of Christ* (Milwaukee: Bruce, 1939).

Jewett, Sophie, *God's Troubadour* (New York: Thomas Y. Crowell Company, 1940).

Kelly, Rev. Wm., *Living for God* (New York: Benziger Brothers, 1948).

Lavelle, Elise, *The Man Who Was Chosen* (New York: McGraw-Hill).

Mannix, Mary, *Illustrated Lives of Patron Saints for Boys and Girls* (New York: Benziger).

Mosely, Daisy, *Sunshine and Saints* (New York: Kenedy, 1935).

Roos, Ann, *Man of Molokai: The Life of Father Damien* (Philadelphia: J. B. Lippincott Co.).

Todd, Mary F., *Song of the Dove* (New York: Kenedy, 1957).

B. Teacher References

Appolonaris, Father, *God's Traffic Lights* (Yonkers, New York: Mission House, 1937).

Baierl, Joseph J., *The Commandments Explained* (St. Paul: Catechetical Guild, 1945).

Butler, Alban, *The Lives of the Saints*, revised by Herbert Thurston and Donald Attwater (New York: Kenedy, 1956).

Cagney, C. P., Alfred, "The Teacher of the Commandments," *Journal of Religious Instruction*, VII, Dec., 1936, pp. 345–354.

Chisholm, Rev. D., *The Catechism in Examples*, Vol. III: *The Commandments* (New York: Benziger Brothers).

Confraternity of Christian Doctrine, *Church History Through Biography* (Paterson, N. J.: St. Anthony Guild).

DeLancy, Selden Peabody, *Married Saints* (New York: Longmans, Green & Co., 1942).

Drinkwater, Rev. F. H., *Teaching the Catechism, Part II, "The Our Father and the Commandments"* (London: Burns, Oates and Washbourne, Ltd., 1936).

—— *Catechism Stories* (Westminster, Md.: Newman Press, 1948).

—— *More Catechism Stories*, A Teacher's Aid Book (Westminster, Md.: Newman Press, 1949).

—— *Twelve and After* (Westminster, Md.: Newman Press, 1948).

Dorcy, Sister Mary Jean, *Our Lady's Feasts* (New York: Sheed & Ward, 1954).

Ellard, G., *Christian Life and Worship* (Milwaukee: Bruce, 1946).

Farrell, Walter, *Companion to the Summa* (New York: Sheed & Ward, 1942).

Filas, Francis L., *The Family for Families* (Milwaukee: Bruce, 1947).

Fouard, Constant, *The Christ: The Son of God* (New York: Longmans, Green & Co., 1944).

Gillis, Rev. James M., *The Ten Commandments* (New York: Paulist Press, 1931).

Goodier, Alban, *The Charity of Jesus Christ* (Notre Dame, Ind.: Grail).

Guyot, G. H., *Scriptural References for Baltimore Catechism* (New York: Wagner, 1946).

Hagan, Rt. Rev. John, *A Compendium of Catechetical Instruction*, VIII (New York: Benziger Brothers, 1928).

Joan, Sister Mary, O.P., and Nona, Sister Mary, O.P., *Guiding Growth in Christian Social Living*, Vol. III (Washington, D. C.: Catholic University, 1946).

Johnson, George, *Better Men for Better Times* (Washington, D. C.: Catholic University, 1944).

Kelly, W., Brogan, H., and Connors, *Poems for the Grades* (New York: Sadlier).

Kerns, J. C., *Life of Blessed Martin de Porres* (New York: Kenedy, 1937).

Kinkead, Rev. Thomas L., *An Explanation of the Baltimore Catechism* (New York: Benziger).

Kirsch, Felix M., O.M.Cap., *Sex Education and Training in Chastity* (New York: Benziger).

Leo XIII, *On Conditions of Labor* (*Rerum Novarum*) (Washington, D. C.: N.C.W.C., 1942).

Marmion, Columba, O.S.B., *Christ, the Life of the Soul* (St. Louis: Herder, 1935).

Mary Catherine, Sister, and Mary Agnesin, Sister, *Teaching the Commandments* (Milwaukee: Bruce).

McHugh, J., *Catechism of the Council of Trent* (New York: Wagner).

The New Testament (Confraternity of Christian Doctrine ed.) (Paterson, N. J.: St. Anthony Guild, 1941).

O'Brien, Isidore, O.F.M., *The Life of Christ* (Paterson, N. J.: St. Anthony Guild Press, 1937).

Old Testament, The (CCD ed. for Pentateuch, Wisdom literature, Prophets, Earlier Historical Books).

O'Rafferty, Nicholas, *The Commandments of God* (Milwaukee: Bruce, 1940).

Pius XI, *Encyclical on the Kingship of Christ* (Washington, D. C.: N.C.W.C., 1929).

Pius XII, encyclical: *Mediator Dei on the Liturgy* (Washington, D. C.: N.C.W.C., 1944).

—— *Encyclical on the Mystical Body* (Washington, D. C.: N.C.W.C., 1943).

—— *The Raccolta* (New York: Benziger, 1943).

Reinhold, H. A., *Our Parish* (New York: Paulist Press, 1943).

School Sisters of Notre Dame, *Teaching the Ten Commandments* (Milwaukee: Bruce, 1931).

Schumacher, Rt. Rev. M., *How to Teach the Catechism*, Vol. II (New York: Benziger, 1945).

Treacy, Gerald C., *Honor God's Name* (New York: Paulist Press, 1940).

C. Materials (Audio-Visual Aids)

FILMSTRIPS:

The Commandments, Society for Visual Education, Inc., Chicago, Illinois.

Honor Thy Father and Thy Mother, Eye Gate House, Inc., Jamaica, N. Y.

UNIT THREE. LIVING THROUGH CHRIST, WITH CHRIST, IN CHRIST

(Text, pp. 180—373)

OUTLINE OF CONTENT

I. **Christ's Sacraments in General**
(Text, pp. 184—196; Baltimore Catechism, Lesson 23)

II. **Christ Incorporates Us Into the Life of His Mystical Body: Baptism**
(Text, pp. 197—213; Baltimore Catechism, Lesson 24)

III. **Christ Strengthens Us to Advance From Supernatural Childhood to Supernatural Maturity: Confirmation**
(Text, pp. 214—227; Baltimore Catechism, Lesson 25)

IV. **Christ Gives Us Himself in Holy Communion Through the Sacrifice of the Mass**
(Text, pp. 228—290; Baltimore Catechism, Lessons 26—28)

V. **Christ Restores or Increases the Life of Grace in Our Soul: Penance and Indulgences**
(Text, pp. 291—353; Baltimore Catechism, Lessons 29—33)

VI. **Christ Prepares the Soul for Eternity in the Sacrament of Extreme Unction**
(Text, pp. 354—374; Baltimore Catechism, Lesson 34)

SECTION I: Christ's Sacraments in General
(Text, pp. 184—196; Baltimore Catechism, Lesson 23)

OUTLINE OF UNIT THREE, SECTION I

A. **A Sacrament Is an Outward Sign Instituted by Christ to Give Grace** (Text, pp. 185—189)

1. **A Sacrament Is an Outward Sign** (Text, pp. 185—186)
2. **Christ Instituted Seven Sacraments** (Text, pp. 186—187)
3. **Source of the Power of the Sacraments** (Text, p. 187)
4. **The Sacraments Give Sanctifying Grace** (Text, pp. 187—188)
5. **The Sacraments Impart Sacramental Grace** (Text, p. 188)
6. **Do the Sacraments Always Give Grace?** (Text, p. 189)

B. **Sacraments Are Classified as the Sacraments of the Dead and of the Living** (Text, pp. 189—191)

C. **Sacraments Received Once; Sacraments Received More Than Once** (Text, pp. 191—192)

TEACHING SUGGESTIONS FOR UNIT THREE, SECTION I

I. OBJECTIVES

A. Primary Objective

To develop a clear understanding and appreciation of the special grace of each sacrament, and to guide the students in the right use of the sacramental graces they receive.

B. Auxiliary Objectives

For the Intellect:

1. To understand the nature and purpose of each of the sacraments, and the conditions required for its worthy reception.
2. To realize how each sacrament brings us the grace of Christ's Redemption to satisfy the needs of supernatural living from birth to death.
3. To understand the meaning of the supernatural life of grace, of the opportunities offered to us and all men to live this life on earth and in heaven.

For the Will:

1. To increase our love for Jesus, Source of all grace, and the determination to grow constantly in the life of grace, in union with Him.
2. To share in the Divine Life of the Church through the reception of the sacraments, especially the sacraments of Penance and Holy Eucharist.

II. NOTES ON TEACHER PRESENTATION

A. Suggestions for Developing Understanding of Subject Matter

1. *Bible story:* Last Supper Discourse (Jn. 15:1–9)
   Discuss:
   How does life enter into the branches?
   What will happen if the branches are cut from the vine?
   Can you see how this carries over to our life in Christ? to God's life in us?
   How do the sacraments bring us this life?
2. Our Lord used external signs on several occasions when He performed miracles.
   Read: Jn. 9:6–7; Mt. 8:15; Mk. 5:41
   What sign was used in each miracle?
   What was the effect?
   Could any of these miracles have been performed without signs? Why?
   Read: Mt. 8:5–13
   Did our Lord use any external signs here?
   Can God give grace without external signs?
3. *Picture study:* Pictures of the administration of the sacraments, the Crucifixion, graph of the Fountain of Life and Rivers of Grace, sacred signs.
   Explain how each sacrament gives a special sacramental grace. Have the pupils observe that the signs are different in each, indicating the different effects of each.
4. Look up the following scriptural texts and show how they prove that Christ instituted the seven sacraments: Acts 13:2–3; James 5:14; Jn. 6:44; Mt. 28:19; Lk. 22:19–20; Mk. 16:6; Eph. 5:25–28; Jn. 7:37–39; 20:19–23.
5. Quotations for discussion and application:
   a) "Without me, you can do nothing."
   b) "Accuse thyself, and God will excuse thee; excuse thyself and God will accuse thee" (St. Augustine).
   c) "By the grace of God, I am what I am" (St. Paul).
   d) "I am come that they may have life, and may have it more abundantly (Jn. 10:10).
6. *Bulletin-board display:* A mural on the chief means of grace, giving central place to the Mass as the fount of supernatural life.

B. Correlating Activities

1. Plan posters or a seven-panel frieze to illustrate the seven sacraments.
2. Tell stories of mission people receiving the sacraments.
3. Choose one sacrament and write about its place in the supernatural life of your own family.
4. Explain to Janice Marie, a non-Catholic, how the seven sacraments meet the spiritual needs of the individual and of the Church.
5. Give from your Bible History three examples of persons who resisted the grace of God; five examples of persons who co-operated with His grace.
6. Report to the class the following incidents: Mk. 7:33–34; Mt. 8:3; Jn. 9:6–7; Jn. 13:4–10; Mt. 8:26.
7. Compose a prayer of thanksgiving for the graces you have received either in Baptism or in Confirmation.
8. From the 42nd psalm, said by the priest at the foot of the altar, select the verse which contains an excellent prayer for the grace of God.
9. Draw and explain symbols of the seven sacraments.
10. Problems for group discussion:
    a) Tim, a non-Catholic, says: "You claim that certain outward signs, or a few words spoken with some other actions, can give spiritual effects which you call grace. How can they do it?" Explain.
    b) Mr. Robertson unfortunately commits a sacrilege by receiving Holy Communion unworthily. Is that a mortal sin? What forms of punishment follow in its wake? He now repents and makes a good confession. Do any penalties still remain? Explain your answer.
    c) Gerald, a happy-go-lucky lad in the eighth grade, wants to know what is the use of going to confession every two weeks, as Father Frank advises the girls and boys to do. Gerald claims he doesn't commit any mortal sins. Tell Gerald why the priest wisely recommends confession frequently.

C. Application

1. Offer prayers and sacrifices that others may benefit from the graces offered by Christ through His Church.
2. Resolve to be reverent and devout toward the sacraments; never to receive them carelessly or through routine.
3. Resolve never to be guilty of the grave sacrilege of receiving a sacrament unworthily.
4. Pray, especially when receiving Holy Communion, that the true Faith may be spread and the sacraments given to all men and to consider your part in it.

Make symbolic posters of the principal means of grace.

Give a scriptural quotation concerning each: the Mass, each of the sacraments, prayer, and sacramentals.

III. EVALUATION

MULTIPLE CHOICE: Choose the one correct answer and print the letter of your choice in the answer space on the right.

1. An outward sign instituted by Christ to give grace is a   1. C
   - A. beatitude
   - B. commandment
   - C. sacrament
   - D. virtue

2. One becomes a member of Christ's Mystical Body by receiving   2. D
   - A. Confirmation
   - B. Penance
   - C. Holy Eucharist
   - D. Baptism

3. Grace is obtained *especially* through   3. A
   - A. use of the sacraments
   - B. sacramentals
   - C. indulgences
   - D. good works

4. "I am the vine, you are the branches. He who abides in Me and I in him, bears much fruit." This refers particularly to   4. D
   - A. actual grace
   - B. sacramental grace
   - C. necessity of good works
   - D. sanctifying grace

5. Baptism and Penance are called sacraments of the dead because they   5. D
   - A. help one carry out the purpose of the sacrament
   - B. imprint on the soul a lasting character
   - C. give more grace to the souls already spiritually alive through sanctifying grace
   - D. bring the supernatural life of sanctifying grace to souls

6. The effectiveness of the grace of the sacraments depends chiefly on   6. C
   - A. the priest who administers them
   - B. God's mercy
   - C. our disposition and co-operation
   - D. the prayer of the Church

7. The greatest gift that Adam and Eve lost in the Garden of Eden was   7. C
   - A. immortality
   - B. strength of the will
   - C. sanctifying grace
   - D. an enlightened understanding

8. The grace that helps us to do good and avoid evil is   8. D
   - A. grace of perseverance
   - B. sacramental grace
   - C. sanctifying grace
   - D. actual grace

9. Sacraments were instituted by   9. C
   - A. Pope
   - B. Apostles
   - C. Christ
   - D. Church

10. The sacrament which contains the body and blood, soul and divinity of Jesus Christ under the appearance of bread and wine is   10. C
    - A. Baptism
    - B. Confirmation
    - C. Holy Eucharist
    - D. Penance

11. The grace of final perseverance   11. D
    - A. remits punishment due to sin
    - B. safeguards against temptations
    - C. obtains pardon for sinners
    - D. enables us to continue in the state of grace until death

12. "Without me you can do nothing" means that   12. D
    - A. we lose merit in state of sin
    - B. we should pray when we receive a sacrament
    - C. everything we do is pleasing to God
    - D. we can do nothing to gain heaven without God's help

13. Reconciliation with God and the remission of eternal punishment are effects of the sacrament of   13. C
    - A. Baptism
    - B. Holy Eucharist
    - C. Penance
    - D. Holy Orders

14. The sacraments that are intended for frequent use are   14. D
    - A. Penance and Baptism
    - B. Matrimony and Penance
    - C. Baptism and Holy Eucharist
    - D. Penance and Holy Eucharist

15. "Amen, amen, I say to thee, unless a man be born again of water and the Spirit, he cannot enter into the kingdom of God." This refers to the sacrament of   15. A
    - A. Baptism
    - B. Holy Orders
    - C. Penance
    - D. Holy Eucharist

16. The most necessary sacrament is   16. D
    - A. Extreme Unction
    - B. Holy Eucharist
    - C. Penance
    - D. Baptism

17. The sacrament containing the Author of all the sacraments is   17. B
    - A. Penance
    - B. Holy Eucharist
    - C. Holy Orders
    - D. Extreme Unction

18. The sacraments receive their power to give grace from   18. D
    - A. the priest
    - B. the prayer of the Church
    - C. our disposition and co-operation
    - D. God

19. "Then they [Peter and John] laid their hands on them [the new converts] and they received the Holy Spirit." This refers to the sacrament of   19. D
    - A. Extreme Unction
    - B. Penance
    - C. Holy Orders
    - D. Confirmation

20. The best means of preserving and strengthening the supernatural life in one's soul is to
   A. listen to the advice of priest, parents, and teachers
   B. avoid bad companions
   C. faithfully say morning and night prayers
   D. go to confession frequently and receive Holy Communion as often as possible

20. D

COMPLETION: Supply the missing word or words which will make the sentence correct. Write the word or words in the corresponding answer space on the right.

1. The supernatural gift bestowed on us through the merits of Jesus Christ for our salvation is (1).

1. sanctifying grace

2. The rewards Christ earned by His sufferings and death are called (2).

2. merits

3. The sacraments were (3) by Jesus Christ.

3. instituted

4. Every sacrament is an (4) sign which imparts (5) as well as sanctifying grace.

4. outward
5. sacramental

5. The supernatural life of the soul is (6).

6. sanctifying grace

6. The principal ways of obtaining grace are (7) and (8).

7. prayer
8. sacraments

7. The sacrament that is called the "Gate of the Church" is (9).

9. Baptism

8. (10) is the usual sacrament that restores sanctifying grace which has been lost by mortal sin.

10. Penance

9. The sin which a person commits when he knowingly receives a sacrament of the living in mortal sin is called (11).

11. sacrilege

10. A spiritual mark imprinted on the soul by three of the sacraments is called a (12).

12. character

11. The sacrament which is a symbol of the union of Christ with His Church is the sacrament of (13).

13. Matrimony

ESSAY

1. What is the meaning of our Lord's words:
   "Lay up to yourselves treasures in heaven: where neither the rust nor moth doth consume, and where thieves do not break through, nor steal."
   What truth is expressed in these words?
   What practices can you suggest to make the truths function in your life and in the lives of others?
2. Explain to Susan, a convert, how the Sacraments of the Living promote our spiritual growth.

IV. ANSWERS TO STUDY EXERCISE FOR UNIT THREE, SECTION I
(Text, pp. 193–194)

I. Multiple Choice (p. 193):

1. B	4. D	7. B	10. D	13. D
2. D	5. C	8. B	11. D	14. D
3. A	6. A	9. C	12. B	15. A

II. Scripture Hunt (p. 194):

Jn. 3:5 — Baptism
1 Cor. 11:23–25 — Holy Eucharist
James 5:14–15 — Extreme Unction
Eph. 5:31 — Matrimony
Mt. 26:22–28 — Holy Eucharist
Jn. 20:23 — Penance
Lk. 22:19 — Holy Eucharist, Holy Orders

SECTION II: Christ Incorporates Us Into the Life of His Mystical Body: Baptism
(Text, pp. 197–213; Baltimore Catechism, Lesson 24)

OUTLINE OF UNIT THREE, SECTION II

A. **Baptism Is a Sacrament of "New Life"** (Text, pp. 198–199)
   1. Baptism Was Instituted by Christ (Text, p. 198)
   2. Baptism Is an Outward Sign (Text, p. 198)
   3. Baptism Confers Grace (Text, pp. 198–199)

B. **Baptism Produces Marvelous Effects in the Soul** (Text, pp. 199–202)
   1. Baptism Takes Away Original and Actual Sins (Text, p. 200)
   2. Baptism Confers Sanctifying Grace (Text, p. 201)
   3. Effects of the Baptismal Character (Text, p. 202)

C. **Baptism Is Administered In and Through the Church** (Text, pp. 202–203)
   1. The Priest Is the Ordinary Minister (Text, p. 202)
   2. Anyone May Baptize (Text, pp. 202–203)

D. **Baptism Is Necessary for Salvation** (Text, pp. 203–206)

E. **Godparents Are Required for Baptism** (Text, pp. 206–207)
   1. Baptismal Promises (Text, p. 207)
   2. The Chief Duty of Godparents (Text, p. 207)

F. **The Name of a Saint Is Given at Baptism** (Text, pp. 208–209)

TEACHING SUGGESTIONS FOR UNIT THREE, SECTION II

I. OBJECTIVES

A. Primary Objective

To engender knowledge of what Baptism does and to arouse love for God in gratitude for this great gift.

B. Auxiliary Objectives

For the Intellect:

1. To increase the children's understanding and appreciation of Baptism and to lead them to praise and love God for His goodness.
2. To develop the determination to grow daily in the life of grace received in Baptism.

3. To give the children some understanding of their duties as children of God in regard to the spread of Faith.
4. To help the children realize the importance of Baptism which makes them living members of the Mystical Body of Christ.

For the Will:

1. To show a return of love by living as God's children should live.
2. To appreciate God's great love in conferring on us through Baptism the dignity of being His children.

II. NOTES ON TEACHER PRESENTATION

A. Suggestions for Developing Understanding of Subject Matter

1. Show the filmstrip — Sacrament of Baptism. Kodachrome slides — Baptism of Christ by John the Baptist.
2. Read carefully Mt. 18:19 and Jn. 3:5 for a better understanding of the text.
3. *Research:* Bible stories on Baptism. Explain the difference between the Baptism given by John the Baptist and that given by the Apostles. Mt. 3:1–12; Acts 8:26–40; Acts 2:14–36; Jn. 3:1–6; Mk. 16:15–16.
4. Read Jn. 3:3. What does Christ teach us concerning Baptism?
5. Read and discuss one of the poems: "Baptism," "God's Priests," "Thy Kingdom Come" (in *Every Child's Garden of Verses*).
6. *Problem for discussion:* Frank has been a very broad-minded father. Born and reared a non-Catholic, he allowed his wife to have all four children baptized and sent to a Catholic school. Edith Ann is now 16 years old. "Your cousin Tom is to be baptized at the Presbyterian Church on Sunday," her father says, "and they have asked you to be a sponsor. I wish you to do this. In fact, I see no reason why you should refuse." Edith Ann must do some talking. What will she do and say? Why?

B. Correlating Activities

1. Write a class letter to a pagan child telling him what Baptism will do for him.
2. Tell stories of the heroism of missionaries at home and abroad to baptize a single person.
3. Report on early martyrs who received the Baptism of desire and of blood.
4. *Group discussion:* Explain how the effects of Baptism reach out through a person's whole life, rather than being limited to the day of one's Baptism.
5. *Bulletin-board-display:* Clippings or written reports concerning modern saints . . . their canonization, their gifts to us of practical examples of holiness, especially those which we can imitate.

6. Conduct a panel discussion on Baptism:
   Baptism, Our Adoption by God
   Baptism, a Measureless Gift
   Baptism, a Pledge of Eternal Life
7. Review how to baptize, in case of necessity; demonstrate an emergency Baptism with a doll.
8. Attend a Baptism in church and follow the ceremonies with the "Rite of Baptism."
9. *Scripture study . . . story hour:* Divide the following references among the class. Let each student or group prepare to tell an interesting story. Report the incident; give an appropriate application and a checkup in the form of discussion questions: Exod. 14:15–22; Zach. 13:1; Jn. 1:6–8; Lk. 1:5–25; Jn. 1:35–39; Acts 2:36–41; 8:26–40; 19:1–7.
10. Write a letter to an imaginary sponsor, explaining his duties at Baptism and afterward.
11. Problems for group discussion:
    a) Jim Turney was studying hard to become a Catholic, for he wanted to save his soul as Christ commanded. One day while swimming he drowned without having been baptized. What chance has he for salvation?
    b) Jo Ann, a non-Catholic, asks you to baptize her. She is twelve years old. May you baptize her? Why? Under what circumstances could you baptize her? What would you consider a "case of necessity"?
    c) The Holy Innocents, martyred by cruel Herod shortly after Jesus was born, are honored by the Church as saints. Did some priest baptize them before they died? Why not? How was original sin removed from their souls? How was sanctifying grace given to them?
12. List the rights and duties that you have as a baptized person.
13. *Meditation:* When you were baptized, you were made a child of God. Our heavenly Father, seeing in you the likeness of His divine Son, was well pleased with you. Think over what God expects of you in your present circumstances as His loving child.
14. Explain briefly why Catholics should frequently renew their baptismal vows.
15. How can you today best prove yourself a loyal, loving child of God?
16. Suggest the opportunities you have today to help the missionaries who are working to bring Baptism to those outside the Kingdom of Christ.

C. Application

1. Make an act of thanksgiving for having been a child of God at Baptism.
2. Pray that others may receive Baptism. Speak often about the necessity of Baptism.
3. Visit Jesus in the Blessed Sacrament and thank Him for the sacrament of Baptism and for all it does for us.

4. Make a sacrifice . . . save pennies for the Holy Childhood Association.
5. Renounce Satan by saying a short ejaculatory prayer every time you are tempted to sin.

III. EVALUATION

MULTIPLE CHOICE: Print the letter of your choice in the answer space on the right.

1. The sacrament that gives us the right to call God our Father is   1. C
   A. Holy Eucharist   C. Baptism
   B. Holy Orders   D. Matrimony

2. Having an ardent wish to receive Baptism and to do all that God has ordained is to have received Baptism of   2. C
   A. blood   B. water   C. desire

3. Anyone may baptize a baby who is   3. C
   A. over two weeks old
   B. sick
   C. in danger of death
   D. over a year old

4. The sponsors for Baptism must be   4. D
   A. non-Catholics   C. good citizens
   B. parish members   D. practical Catholics

5. The promises at Baptism are made by   5. D
   A. the parents of the child
   B. the child
   C. the foster parents
   D. the godparents

6. Baptism makes us members of the   6. C
   A. Church Triumphant   C. Church
   B. sodality   D. congregation

7. If parents put off the Baptism of one of their children for a long time they commit   7. B
   A. a sacrilege   C. venial sin
   B. a mortal sin   D. no sin

8. A person who suffers death unjustly inflicted, in testimony of his Faith or for a Christian virtue, receives the baptism of   8. B
   A. desire   B. blood   C. water

ESSAY

1. Write a letter to a boy in Korea telling him:
   a) Why the sacrament of Baptism is most important.
   b) How the sacrament is administered.
   c) How he could administer the sacrament in an emergency.
2. Write a short life of your patron saint. Tell how your patron showed love of God and love of neighbor.
3. What are some of the rights and duties you have as a baptized person?

IV. ANSWERS TO STUDY EXERCISES FOR UNIT THREE, SECTION II
(Text, pp. 209–210)

I. A "Because Test" (pp. 209–210):
Answers may vary.

1. In case of necessity he may have to baptize.
2. The person bearing the name should have someone to imitate.
3. Christ said: "Unless a man be born again of water and the Holy Spirit, he cannot enter into the kingdom of God."
4. They are children of God.
5. It is the duty of godparents to know the true Faith, live up to the duties of their religion, and bring the children up as good Catholics.
6. Without Baptism no one can enter heaven.
7. He is in the state of sanctifying grace.
8. Christ had not instituted the sacrament as yet.
9. They are responsible for the upbringing of the children in the Catholic religion if the child's parents die or fail to live up to their responsibilities.
10. Neither imprints the special character of the sacrament on the soul.

II. Completion (p. 210):
1. heaven
2. the priest
3. "I baptize thee in the name of the Father and of the Son and of the Holy Ghost."
4. to be a practical Catholic
5. baptism of blood

SECTION III: Christ Strengthens Us to Advance From Supernatural Childhood to Supernatural Maturity: Confirmation
(Text, pp. 214–227; Baltimore Catechism, Lesson 25)

OUTLINE OF UNIT THREE, SECTION III

A. The Full Spiritual Growth to Perfection Is the Purpose and Effect of Confirmation (Text, pp. 214–219)
1. Confirmation Was Instituted by Christ (Text, pp. 215–216)
2. Confirmation Has an Outward Sign (Text, pp. 216–217)
3. The Effects of Confirmation Are Threefold (Text, pp. 218–219)

B. The Church Teaches Us How to Receive Confirmation Properly (Text, pp. 219–220)

C. As Confirmed Persons We Have Additional Responsibilities (Text, p. 220)

TEACHING SUGGESTIONS FOR UNIT THREE, SECTION III

I. OBJECTIVES

A. Primary Objective

To build up in students a realization of the role Confirmation has to play in our Christ-life.

B. Auxiliary Objectives

For the Intellect:

1. To increase our knowledge of the sacrament of Confirmation, which strengthens our faith and prepares us for warfare against our spiritual enemies.
2. To increase understanding and appreciation of what it means to be a "soldier of Christ."
3. To develop appreciation of the spiritual favors received through the sacrament.

For the Will:

1. To profess our belief through Christlike living.
2. To arouse an eager desire to use the special graces of Confirmation for our own growth in the supernatural life and for the welfare of others.

II. NOTES ON TEACHER PRESENTATION

A. Suggestions for Developing Understanding of Subject Matter

1. View the filmstrip: *Sacrament of Confirmation.*
2. Discuss the possibility of a pupil's being a good student, an excellent athlete, and at the same time a real Catholic Action leader.
3. *Stories:* Coming of the Holy Spirit (Acts 2:1–13); the Apostles after the death of Jesus (Jn. 20:19); the Apostles after the coming of the Holy Spirit (Acts 2:14–41).
4. *Picture study:* Picture of Apostles administering Confirmation to early Christians. Note the imposition of hands (Acts 8:14–17). Picture of a bishop administering Confirmation.
5. *Bulletin-board display:* Pictures of missionaries, of martyrs, men and women of today who have professed their faith in the face of hardships and death.
6. Invite a priest or missionary to speak on Catholic Action.
7. Read 1 Cor. 13:11. In what way do these words of St. Paul express the effects of Confirmation?
8. Interpret the following quotations: 2 Tim. 2:3; Mt. 32. Is there a lesson for us? Why?
9. *Problem for discussion:* The Judd family have just moved to the East from Colorado. The only people whom they know are the Prangles, who are not Catholic. Joan Judd is to receive the Sacrament of Confirmation. "Judy Prangle will be your sponsor," Mrs. Judd decides. "We do not know anyone else in the city. Besides, the Prangles have been very good to us since we came here. What difference does it make?" Perhaps you can explain.
10. *Research:* In the sacrament of Confirmation we are sealed as apostles of Christ, co-workers with Him in His work of bringing men to His heavenly Father. This is work not only for grownups. Children of your age have been real apostles of Christ. Report how each of these saints, as children, helped to bring others into the kingdom of God: St. John Bosco, St. Bernadette, St. Therese, St. Madeline Sophie, St. Agnes, St. Catherine of Siena, St. Dominic Savio, St. Maria Goretti.

B. Correlating Activities

1. "The greatest enemy of Christ is ignorance of Christ." What could you and your classmates do to defeat this enemy of Christ? *Discuss.*
2. Present a choral reading with musical background of the "Hymn to the Holy Spirit."
3. Write a letter to a child who has not received Confirmation. Explain how we receive this sacrament, and what its benefits are.
4. Collect for the bulletin board newspaper pictures and articles of men and women who are active Catholic leaders.
5. Read the sequence from the Mass of the feast of Pentecost. Be able to pick out the numerous petitions which the Church makes in this hymn for us.
6. Relate the use of graces received in Confirmation to the persecuted yet loyal Catholics of Europe and Asia.
7. Collect pictures from mission magazines; discuss the growth of the Church in mission lands and at home.
8. *Discuss:* In what circumstances of your present life do you need the sacramental grace of Confirmation?
9. Give one-minute talks on the following topics:
   Martyrdom of St. Sebastian
   Martyrdom of St. Agnes
   Martyrdom of St. Tarcisius
   Modern martyrs of Russia, Mexico, Spain, Hungary
10. Panel discussion:
   a) In the sacrament of Confirmation we receive the Holy Spirit, to make us apostles of Christ and to enable us to carry on our part in His sanctifying activities. How would vigorous, faithful co-operation with the grace of the Holy Spirit manifest itself in young people of your age today? What opportunities have you for participating in Catholic Action?
   b) As an apostle of Christ through Confirmation, discuss:
      1) How you can advance the reign of Christ within you today; and
      2) By what specific acts you can help to extend the reign of Christ among men in all corners of the world.
11. Show how in the following prayer to the Holy Spirit we ask for something that is more necessary for the adult Christian than it is for the infant Christian: "Increase in our souls, O Holy Spirit, Thy divine gifts which as blessed instincts of grace mercifully impel us to approve the better things."

12. Dramatize incidents in the lives of the following saints, and ask the class "Who am I?" St. Isaac Jogues, St. Paul, St. Stephen, St. Rose of Lima, St. John the Baptist, St. Louis of France, St. Vincent de Paul.

13. Read the letter of Pope Pius XII to children of the United States wherein he appealed for both spiritual and temporal help for the suffering of all nations.

C. Application

1. Uphold truth and virtue at all times as becomes a soldier of Christ.

2. Be an example among our companions in all matters regarding truth, honesty, purity.

3. Follow Jesus as a true soldier by obeying the Commandments of God in daily life and giving a good example to others.

4. Pray for all those who do not have the true Faith.

III. EVALUATION

ESSAY:

1. Why should Catholics continue to study their religion even more earnestly after they have received the sacrament of Confirmation?

2. Two things are necessary for salvation: to know the will of God, and to do it. Show how the Seven Gifts of the Holy Ghost help us to this end.

3. Explain the meaning of Catholic Action in the life of an eighth grader.

COMPLETION: Supply the missing word or words which will make the sentence correct. Write the answers in the spaces provided.

1. Confirmation may be given to all Catholics not yet confirmed. To receive the Sacrament of Confirmation one must (1) and (2).

2. Usually Confirmation is administered by the (3).

3. The sacramental grace of Confirmation helps us to (4).

4. Confirmation is the Sacrament through which we (5) to enable us to (6) as strong and (7) Christians.

5. Confirmation increases (8), gives its (9) grace, and (10) a lasting (11) on the soul.

1. be in the state of grace
2. know well the chief truths and duties of our religion
3. bishop
4. live our faith loyally and to profess it courageously
5. receive the Holy Ghost
6. live
7. perfect
8. sanctifying grace
9. special sacramental
10. imprints
11. character

6. When the bishop confirms he says: "I (12) and I (13) in the name of (14)."

7. Holy chrism is a mixture of (15) and is blessed by the (16) on (17).

8. The (18) comes to us in a special way in the sacrament of Confirmation.

9. As confirmed persons we have certain responsibilities, e.g., to (19) and (20).

12. sign thee with the sign of the cross
13. confirm thee with the chrism of salvation
14. the Father, and of the Son, and of the Holy Ghost
15. olive oil and balm
16. Bishop
17. Holy Thursday
18. Holy Spirit
19. explain and defend our Faith
20. to co-operate with the grace of Confirmation

IV. ANSWERS TO STUDY EXERCISE FOR UNIT THREE, SECTION III
(Text, p. 221)

Completion (p. 221):

1. bishop
2. Holy Ghost
3. chrism
4. soldier
5. living

ANSWERS TO ACHIEVEMENT TEST FOR UNIT THREE, SECTIONS I, II, and III (Text, pp. 224–227)

I. Completion (pp. 224–225):

1. (sanctifying) grace
2. right dispositions
3. sacraments of the dead
4. sacrament
5. Baptism
6. bishop
7. chrism
8. Holy Thursday
9. sacramental grace
10. character
11. Christ
12. baptism of blood
13. Confirmation
14. matter
15. form
16. godparents
17. Catholics
18. religion
19. baptism of desire
20. anointing
21. faith
22. practice
23. merits
24. Catholic Action
25. sanctifying grace

II. Yes or No (p. 226):

1. Yes	6. No	11. Yes	16. No	21. Yes
2. Yes	7. Yes	12. No	17. Yes	22. No
3. No	8. Yes	13. No	18. No	23. Yes
4. No	9. No	14. Yes	19. Yes	24. No
5. Yes	10. Yes	15. No	20. Yes	25. No

SECTION IV: Christ Gives Us Himself in Holy Communion Through the Sacrifice of the Mass

(Text, pp. 228–290; Baltimore Catechism, Lesson 26)
Part One. The Holy Eucharist and the Mass

OUTLINE OF UNIT THREE, SECTION IV

A. The Holy Eucharist Is a Sacrament and a Sacrifice (Text, p. 229)

B. The Institution of the Holy Eucharist Took Place at the Last Supper (Text, pp. 232–234)

C. Transubstantiation (Text, pp. 234–238)

D. Christ Gave to Priests the Power to Change Bread and Wine Into His Body and Blood (Text, pp. 238–239)

E. Christ Gives Us His Own Body and Blood in the Holy Eucharist for Many Reasons (Text, pp. 239–241)

TEACHING SUGGESTIONS FOR UNIT THREE, SECTION IV, PART ONE — The Holy Eucharist

I. OBJECTIVES

A. Primary Objective

To help one understand and realize the relationship between the Holy Eucharist as a Sacrifice and a Sacrament.

B. Auxiliary Objectives

For the Intellect:

1. To develop a fuller understanding and appreciation of this sacrament, the greatest gift of God's love and mercy.
2. To realize that the Holy Eucharist is a sacrament and sacrifice.
3. To increase our knowledge and appreciation of the effects of Holy Communion.

For the Will:

1. To develop a deep reverence and love for Jesus in the Holy Eucharist.
2. To acquire the habit of frequent and devout reception of Holy Communion.
3. To increase our love for Jesus and gratitude to Him; to develop an appreciation and reverence for the priesthood.

II. NOTES ON TEACHER PRESENTATION

A. Suggestions for Developing Understanding of Subject Matter

1. View the filmstrip: *The Holy Eucharist.*
2. Tell the class how the miracle of Christ walking on the water (Mt. 14:22–23) was to prepare the Apostles for the astounding promise of which St. John tells us in Chapter 6, verses 22–72.
3. Read or select several students to make a class report on Christ's promise of the Holy Eucharist after the Multiplication of the Loaves (Jn. 6). Discuss.

4. Tell the story of what happened at the Last Supper. Give the details by answering the questions: Who? What? When? Why? How?
5. In the Holy Eucharist Jesus Christ is present, is offered, and is consumed by us. Show that the following prayer states the reason why Christ gave us the Holy Eucharist: "O Sacred Banquet in which Christ is received, the memory of His Passion is kept, the mind is filled with grace, and there is given to us a pledge of future glory."
6. Read the three prayers of preparation for Holy Communion said by the priest in the Mass. For what do we ask in each? Why are these prayers the best we can say before Holy Communion?
7. *Problem for discussion:* A boy doesn't receive Holy Communion very often because he is afraid other boys will laugh at him. What thought would help him to overcome his fear?

B. Correlating Activities

1. *Discuss:* Why is the Holy Eucharist the most excellent of all the sacraments? Why is it called the Sacrament of Love?
2. Draw some of the more common symbols of the Eucharist.
3. Examine the prayer: "O God, Who in this wonderful Sacrament . . ." which the priest sings at Benediction. What do we learn about the Blessed Sacrament in this prayer? For what do we pray?
4. Plan a bulletin board with pictures, symbols, poems on the Holy Eucharist.
5. Sing songs in honor of Jesus in the Blessed Sacrament.
6. Suggest some ejaculations which could be said by a person genuflecting before the Blessed Sacrament.
7. Write a brief composition on "Eucharistic Congresses." Describe the "Forty Hours' Devotion" as held at your church.
8. Make a report on the feast of Corpus Christi. How did this feast originate? Who wrote the great Eucharistic hymns?
9. What is your answer?
   a) A non-Catholic friend of yours wants to know why we teach that the Holy Eucharist is present only in Catholic churches and chapels?
   b) A boy taking instructions wants to know how the manna in the desert prefigured the Holy Eucharist.
10. *Group discussion:* Our privilege of receiving the Holy Eucharist frequently and daily. Our obligation of preparing properly for receiving.
11. Examine the following prayers. What effects of Holy Communion are referred to in each. See how the promise made by Christ after the miracle of the loaves is gloriously fulfilled in the Holy Eucharist.

      Secret — Sunday in Octave of Corpus Christi

Postcommunion — Third Sunday after Easter

Postcommunion — Sixth Sunday after Epiphany

Postcommunion — Twenty-First Sunday after Pentecost

12. Write a paragraph expressing thanksgiving after Communion.

13. Learn the prayer "Soul of Christ" and pray it often, especially after Holy Communion.

14. Explain: A lifetime would not be long enough for us to give adequate thanks to God for the gifts of one Holy Communion.

15. Read in your Missal from the Mass of next Sunday the Communion prayer. What reference has it to Holy Communion? Read the Postcommunion. For what grace do we pray in this prayer?

16. Problems for discussion:

a) Ronald, a convert, wants to know how he can continue his thanksgiving for Holy Communion throughout the day.

b) Joseph is kneeling at the altar and ready to receive Holy Communion when he remembers that he is in the state of mortal sin. What should he do?

c) Your little brother asks you to explain to him what is meant by a spiritual communion. How often should he make a spiritual communion?

d) Father John encourages the boys and girls to receive Holy Communion frequently, daily if possible. Why?

17. *Meditation:* Consider, if we had been with the multitude when Jesus promised the Holy Eucharist, whether we would have had enough faith to remain with Him. Ask Him for the grace always to be loyal to Him.

C. Application

1. Believe that in the Holy Eucharist our Lord is contained, offered, and received.

2. Be reverential to Jesus in the Blessed Sacrament at all times.

3. Resolve to receive Holy Communion frequently and devoutly, i.e. every day or week if possible, but at least once a month throughout my entire life.

III. EVALUATION

Matching: Match each item in Column I with an item in Column II and print the letter of your choice in the answer blank on the right.

Column I	Column II	
1. Christ's sacrifice on Mt. Calvary.	A. Holy Eucharist	1. C
		2. E
2. The change of bread and wine into the Body and Blood of Christ	B. Holy Thursday	3. I
		4. G

3. Receiving Jesus Christ

4. The Sacrifice which continues Christ's Sacrifice for all time

5. The offering of bread and wine in the Mass

6. The day before Jesus died

7. Occasion on which Christ instituted the Holy Eucharist

8. Holy Communion for the dying

9. Jesus Christ Himself under the appearances of bread and wine

10. When bread and wine are consecrated in the Mass

C. Sacrifice of the Cross	5. H
D. Last Supper	6. B
E. Transubstantiation	7. D
F. Viaticum	8. F
G. Sacrifice of the Mass	9. A
H. Offertory	10. J
I. Communion	
J. Consecration	

Essay Questions:

1. Explain:

a) What the Holy Eucharist should mean to a child.

b) How I should show my great appreciation for this great gift of God.

c) How God wants me to use this gift.

2. Explain:

a) How the Holy Eucharist unites me to Christ.

b) How it increases sanctifying grace.

c) How it lessens evil inclinations.

3. Write a short composition on:

a) Why I should make a good preparation before Holy Communion.

b) Why I should make a good thanksgiving after Holy Communion.

4. Write a paragraph on the topic: "Why I Should Receive Holy Communion Frequently."

IV. ANSWERS TO STUDY EXERCISES FOR UNIT THREE, SECTION IV, PART ONE
(Text, pp. 242–243)

I. Matching (p. 242):

1. C   2. E   3. B   4. A   5. D

II. Short Answer (pp. 242–243):

1. Last Supper
2. Holy Eucharist
3. Forgiveness of sin
4. the Apostles
5. His Apostles
6. bread
7. wine
8. priests
9. Consecration
10. "This is My Body" "This is My Blood"

III. Missing Words (p. 243):

1. (a) bread, (b) eat, (c) body, (d) wine, (e) drink, (f) blood, (g) sins, (h) apostles, (i) Do

2. (a) sacrament, (b) sacrifice, (c) body, (d) blood, (e) soul, (f) divinity

3. (a) commemorating, (b) renewing, (c) Holy Communion, (d) altars

SECTION IV: Christ Gives Us Himself in Holy Communion Through the Sacrifice of the Mass

(Text, pp. 247–278; Baltimore Catechism, Lesson 27)
Part Two. The Holy Sacrifice of the Mass

OUTLINE OF UNIT III, SECTION IV

A. The Mass Is a Perfect Sacrifice (Text, pp. 247–254)

B. The Mass of the Catechumens Is the Mass of Preparation (Text, pp. 254–260)
   1. We Speak to God (Text, pp. 254–257)
   2. God Speaks to Us (Text, pp. 257–260)

C. The Mass of the Faithful is the Mass of Sacrifice (Text, pp. 260–270)
   1. We Offer Christ and Ourselves (Text, pp. 260–262)
   2. The Sacrifice (Text, pp. 262–266)
   3. We Receive (Text, pp. 266–270)

D. We Should Live the Mass (Text, p. 271)

TEACHING SUGGESTIONS FOR UNIT THREE, SECTION IV, PART TWO — The Mass

I. OBJECTIVES

A. Primary Objective

To realize that the Mass is a Sacrifice in which we offer ourselves to God, with Christ, in order to live in accordance with His holy will.

B. Auxiliary Objectives

For the Intellect:

1. To understand the infinite value of the Sacrifice of the Mass, source of our Redemption and fountain of grace.
2. To understand and appreciate what the Mass is and to realize that offering the Mass is the greatest act one can perform.
3. To realize that the Mass is a sacrifice in which we offer ourselves to God, with Christ, in order to live in accordance with His holy will.
4. To understand what it means to live the Mass.

For the Will:

1. To increase our love for Christ, our Eucharistic Victim.
2. To acquire a greater desire to participate as fully as possible in the Holy Sacrifice.
3. To have the attitude that hearing Mass is a perfect preparation for Holy Communion.
4. To grow in appreciation and devotion in offering the Holy Sacrifice.

II. NOTES FOR TEACHER PRESENTATION

A. Suggestions for Developing Understanding of Subject Matter

1. Show the Kodachrome slides or filmstrip on the Mass.
2. Briefly review the value of the Old Testament sacrifices. Read and discuss: Ps. 39:7–9; Mal. 1:10–11; Ps. 109:4; Hebr. 9:11–14.

Show that the sacrifices of the Old Testament had only a figurative, typical character in preparation for the one Sacrifice of the New Law.

3. Show from Hebr. 11:2–12, how the sacrifice of our Saviour on the Cross replaced all the sacrifices of the old Law.

   Read the scriptural passages to prove that the Sacrifice of the Cross is called the sacrifice of redemption: 1 Pet. 1:19; 1 Cor. 6:20; Apoc. 5:9.

4. Read the prophecy of Malachias 1:11. *Discuss:* What words from this text foretell that there was to be a new sacrifice?

   That it would be offered in every place.

   That it would be a different sacrifice.

   That it would be an unbloody sacrifice.

   That it would be offered by the Gentiles.

   Show that the Mass fulfills this prophecy.

5. Describe how Christ instituted the Blessed Sacrament the night before He died.

   With what words did Christ command the Apostles to offer the Sacrifice of the Mass in remembrance of Himself?

   Compare the three Gospel accounts of Mt. 26:26–28; Mk. 14:22–24; and Lk. 22:19–20, with St. Paul — 1 Cor. 11:23–25, and the consecration narrative of the Missal.

6. Draw a parallel between the sacrifice of Christ on Calvary and the altar.

   To show how the Mass is the renewal or re-enactment of the Sacrifice of Calvary draw this comparison:

   Calvary . . . Source and Reservoir of Graces
   Mass . . . Channels of These Graces

   To reinforce the idea, use the text 1 Cor. 11:26.

7. List on the blackboard in three parallel columns the essential factors that are identical in the Sacrifice of Calvary, the Last Supper, and the Mass.

8. Read our Lord's Prayer for His Apostles in Jn. 17:1–26. Tell what our Lord says of His Sacrifice and of its purpose.

9. Study, compare, and discuss charts and other illustrations of the Mass.

10. Interpret the following quotation: "All that He has, all that He is, He gives; all that we are, all that we have, He takes."

    Why are these words true? What do they teach us about the Mass?

B. Correlating Activities

1. Make a frieze or mural to show how the altar is the center of life and worship for our parish family.

2. Tell how the Mass fulfills the four ends of prayer; how it exemplifies God's best gift to us, and our best gift to God.

3. Draw some conclusions about our participation in the Mass from a consideration of these passages quoted in the texts: Exod. 23:15, 19, 30; Deut. 16:16–17; Ecclus. 25:2.

4. Do you agree with this statement of St. Francis of Assisi: "We know only as much as we do." Discuss whether those who fail to assist at Mass frequently really know the Mass.

5. Find various prayers in the Mass which teach us love, humility, unselfishness, and other Christian virtues.

6. Collect stories and pictures to illustrate the truth that love is always expressed in sacrifice.

7. Select a group of eight to discuss, under the leadership of a chairman, "The Mass, the center of Catholic life in our parish."

8. Can you prove the truth of this statement: "A Christian will become a saint if he earnestly lives the Liturgical Year."

9. Will the following rule help you to apply the principle of living the Mass: "Work as if everything depended on yourself: pray as if everything depended on God"? Why?

10. Give five concrete examples of what you would expect of a boy or girl who lives the Mass.

11. Explain to Alice, a convert, that offering the Mass will let her realize the statement of St. Augustine: "Christ desires you, not your gifts."

12. Conduct a group discussion on the topic: "Which Part of the Mass Means Most to Me."

13. List in your notebook in two columns the parts of the Mass that change from day to day, and the parts that always remain the same. Head them as "The Ordinary of the Mass" and "The Proper of the Mass."

14. Write a paragraph encouraging frequent attendance at Mass; use the argument that every one of us should be there lest Christ's Mystical Body be lacking a member.

15. Discuss the various attitudes toward Sunday Mass taken by the following:

    a) Karl attends Mass for the sole purpose of having his prayer heard — he wants to be promoted to a higher and better paid job.

    b) Ethel attends Mass merely in order not to be guilty of mortal sin, with the risk of going to hell.

    c) Frank offers the Mass primarily because he wants to offer to God a sacrifice worthy of Him, and because in the Mass he can unite himself with Christ in His Sacrifice.

    d) Rose attends Mass because she would be ashamed to confess missing Mass in her next confession.

    Which person has the best motive? Why? Why do you think that the other persons have the wrong attitude for attending Mass? Which one is likely to receive the most graces from God? the least? Why?

16. Make a poster to illustrate that in the Mass Christ continues to offer Himself to His Father; that the priest places his hands beneath the hands of Christ offering Himself; and the laity on their part clasp their hands about the hands

of the offering priest. Discuss the poster with the class.

17. Write a letter to Tim, a convert, and explain why the Mass is a drama in which each of us is an actor.

18. What use can you make of the following lines by James Russell Lowell to prove the need of giving ourselves in the Mass?

    "Not what we give but what we share —
      For the gift without the giver is bare;
    Who gives himself with his alms feeds three—
      Himself, his hungering neighbor, and Me."

19. Read Cardinal Wiseman's *Fabiola*. Report what the Mass meant to the early Christians.

20. Compile a class book on the liturgy to be built up throughout the year; include description and illustrations on the Mass, the Church Year, liturgical vestments, and symbols.

21. Arrange for floor talks on certain people who loved the Mass, e.g., the Christians of the Catacombs, the Irish people during the days of English persecution.

C. Application

1. Assist at Mass intelligently, devoutly, and fruitfully.

2. Assist at Mass and receive Holy Communion daily, if possible.

3. Offer the Mass for various members of the Church Militant and Suffering.

4. Pray for the missionaries who bring the Mass to those who need it.

5. Give something from my allowance or from my earnings for the Propagation of the Faith, which provides every necessity for Holy Mass for the missions.

6. Ask our divine Lord to strengthen my courage that I may say "No" when tempted to sin.

7. Attend Mass with strong faith and devotion in thanksgiving for God's goodness in giving Himself in the Holy Eucharist.

III. EVALUATION

Choose any number of topics and write brief explanations.

1. "The Mass is the means whereby children of God are brought actively into the eternal life of love of the Blessed Trinity."

2. "Daily Mass gives me the opportunity of sharing in the Last Supper, of kneeling on Mt. Calvary with our Lady and St. John."

3. What do you think G. K. Chesterton meant when he said: "It is the Mass that makes men men"?

4. "The Mass, the center of Catholic life in our parish."

5. "From the Sacrifice-Banquet, children of God must go forth to a life of love in the world, to a charity which is all-embracing for the sake of Christ."

6. Why is the Mass the one supreme act of religion that is truly worthy of God?

7. "In the Mass of the Catechumens we speak to God

and God speaks to us; in the Mass of the faithful, we give to God and He gives to us."

Problems for Discussion

1. Elmer asks you whether it is advisable to make the Way of the Cross or to say the Rosary while assisting at Mass.
2. Robert asks you to explain to him why the priest kisses the altar, and how often; and why he extends his hands when he says, *Dominus vobiscum.*
3. Eileen asks why it is appropriate for the people to say the same prayer as the priest says before the Gospel.
4. Can you tell Walter the reason why people should attend the Sunday Mass at which a sermon is preached?
5. Mary Ann came in to the church last Sunday when the priest was saying the *Credo.* Was Mary Ann late for Mass? Did she miss Mass?
6. Orville, a non-Catholic, cannot understand why the Last Supper was the first Mass. Explain that it was.
7. Tom is puzzled about the statement that the Offertory, the Consecration, and the Communion must be included in the Sacrifice of the Mass. Explain.
8. Do you agree with John who says that the Mass is a drama in which we may be more intimately active than were the Apostles at the Last Supper, or at the Crucifixion. Why?
9. If a non-Catholic asked you what benefits you obtain from Mass, what would you answer?
10. Richard says: "No sissy ever became a saint." Do you agree with him? Why?
11. Mark, a non-Catholic, says it is useless to pray for the departed.
12. Alberta cannot understand how we offer the Mass "In Him and with Him and through Him." Can you tell her?
13. George asks you to tell him what is meant by living the Mass all-day long. Tell George.
14. Arthur says he finds it impossible to forgive the injury that Joe has done him. What petition of the Our Father should show Arthur that he is condemning himself? Explain that petition to him.
15. Norman says that perfect assistance at Mass calls for our reception of Holy Communion. Do you agree? Why?
16. Anna contends that one gets more benefit out of the Mass by saying the Rosary. Do you agree with Anna? Why?

SUGGESTION: Divide the class into groups. Hold each group responsible for one or two problems.

IV. ANSWERS TO STUDY EXERCISES FOR UNIT THREE, SECTION IV, PART TWO

(Text, pp. 273–274)

I. Proper Sequence (p. 273):

1. Confiteor	3. Kyrie	5. Collect	7. Gospel
2. Introit	4. Gloria	6. Epistle	8. Credo

II. Matching (p. 273):

1. C	3. E	5. F	7. B	9. D
2. I	4. G	6. H	8. A	

III. Yes or No (p. 273):

1. Yes	3. No	5. No	7. No	9. Yes
2. Yes	4. No	6. No	8. Yes	10. Yes

IV. Matching (p. 274):

1. E	3. B	5. G	7. C
2. D	4. F	6. A	8. H

REFERENCES AND MATERIALS

UNIT THREE, SECTION IV, PART TWO — THE MASS

A. Pupil References

Bussard, Rev. Paul, *If I Be Lifted Up* (St. Paul, Minn.: The Catechetical Guild).

Dooley, Rev. Lester M., *Hello Halo* (Boston: Lumen Press).

Dunney, Rev. Joseph, *The Mass for Boys and Girls* (New York: Macmillan, 1948).

Fitzpatrick, Edward A., *Highway to God*, Highway to Heaven Series, Books VII and VIII (Milwaukee: Bruce, 1939).

—— *The Holy Sacrifice of the Mass*, Highway to Heaven Series, Book VI (Milwaukee: Bruce).

Gasparri, Peter Cardinal, *Catholic Faith III* (New York: Kenedy).

Michel, Dom Virgil, *The Redeeming Sacrifice*, Christ-Like Series, Book V (New York: Macmillan).

B. Teacher References

Adam, Karl, *The Spirit of Catholicism* (New York: Macmillan, 1936). Image Book also available.

Baierl, *Holy Sacrifice of the Mass* (Rochester, N. Y.: Seminary Press).

Bussard and Kirsch, *The Meaning of the Mass* (New York: Kenedy, 1942).

Chery, *What is the Mass?* (Westminster, Md.: Newman, 1952).

Dalgairns, Rev. J. B., *The Holy Communion*, Vol. I, Chap. III (St. Louis: Herder).

D'Arcy, M., *The Mass and the Redemption* (New York: Benziger).

Ellard, Gerald, *Christian Life and Worship*, rev. ed. (Milwaukee: Bruce, 1940).

Farrell, Walter, *Companion to the Summa*, Vol. IV (New York: Sheed & Ward, 1942).

Fortescue, *The Mass. A Study of the Roman Liturgy* (New York: Longmans, 1957).

Gihr, Nicholas, *The Holy Sacrifice of the Mass*, Chap. II (St. Louis: Herder, 1939).

Hellrigel, Martin, *The Holy Sacrifice of the Mass* (St. Louis: Pio Decimo Press, 1944).

Kessler, W. G., *Your Mass Visible* (Dubuque, Iowa: Columbia Museum and Inst. of Art) (Pamphlet).

Kirsch, Felix, and Brendan, Sister M., *Catholic Faith Explored* Book III (Washington, D. C.: Catholic University of America Press).

Lallou-Josefita, *The Missal and Holy Mass* (New York: Benziger).

Lebbe, *The Mass* (Westminster, Md.: Newman, 1949).

Le Febvre, *How to Understand the Mass* (St. Paul, Minn.: Lohmann).

Marmion, Columba, *Christ in His Mysteries* (St. Louis: Herder, 1958).

Montessori, Marie, *Mass Explained to Boys and Girls* (New York: Sadlier, 1934).

Parsch, Pius, *The Liturgy of the Mass* (St. Louis: Herder, 1937).

Pius XII, *On the Sacred Liturgy* (Washington, D. C.: N.C.W.C., 1942) (Pamphlet).

Putz, Joseph, *My Mass* (Westminster, Md.: Newman Press).

Roguet, *Holy Mass: Approaches to the Mystery* (Collegeville, Minn.: Liturgical Press, 1953).

Secular Priest, *A Simple Explanation of Low Mass*, Second Ed. (New York: Kenedy).

Sheen, F., *Calvary and the Mass* (New York: Kenedy).

Spirago-Baxter, *Anecdotes and Examples for the Catechism* (New York: Benziger, 1921).

Sullivan, John, *The Visible Church* (New York: Kenedy).

Vonier, Anscar, *Key to the Doctrine of the Eucharist* (Westminster, Md.: Newman Press).

Zundel, Maurice, *Splendors of the Liturgy* (New York: Sheed & Ward).

C. Materials (Audio-Visual Aids)

FILMSTRIPS:

Prayer and the Mass, Society for Visual Education, Chicago, Ill.

The Mass and the Sacraments, Eye Gate House, Inc., Jamaica, N. Y.

The Holy Mass, Encyclopaedia Britannica Films, 1150 Wilmette Ave., Wilmette, Ill.

SECTION IV: Christ Gives Himself to Us in Holy Communion Through the Sacrifice of the Mass

(Text, pp. 278–290; Baltimore Catechism, Lesson 28) Part Three. Holy Communion — God's Gift to Us

OUTLINE OF UNIT III, SECTION IV

A. Holy Communion Should Be Worthily Received (Text, pp. 279–280)

B. Holy Communion Makes Us More Christlike (Text, pp. 281–286)

TEACHING SUGGESTIONS FOR UNIT THREE, SECTION IV, PART THREE — Holy Communion

I. OBJECTIVES

A. Primary Objective

To realize that in Holy Communion we unite ourselves with Christ in His great Sacrifice.

B. Auxiliary Objectives

For the Intellect:
To learn how to receive Holy Communion.

For the Will:
To learn how to profit from receiving Communion.

II. NOTES FOR TEACHER PRESENTATION

A. Suggestions for Developing Understanding of Subject Matter

1. Discuss picture on page 278 of Text.
2. Discuss food for body; food for soul.
3. Relate Holy Communion to the Mass — receiving the Victim and uniting ourselves with Him and His sacrifice.
4. Discuss the requirements for worthy reception of Holy Communion.
5. Talk over the new requirements for fasting — get them clear.

B. Correlating Activities

1. Discuss and act out proper, courteous, devout behavior in going to the communion rail.
2. Have pupils illustrate how to go to Holy Communion: eyes closed, head up, mouth properly opened, tongue properly out, head not moving, etc., etc.
3. After Communion: brief wait at rail so as not to bump next person while priest is giving him Holy Communion, devout return to seat; what to do after Communion.

C. Application

In Communion I make my closest contact with God on earth. Holy Communion properly received can make me a great saint. Communion should make me Christlike in my dealings with others.

III. EVALUATION

Completion: Supply the missing word or words. Place your answer in the column at the right.

1. Christ instituted Holy Communion to supply our souls with spiritual (1).   1. food
2. In certain Old Testament sacrifices the worshipers were given part of the victim to (2).   2. eat
3. To receive Holy Communion worthily a person must be free from (3), have a right (4), and obey the Church's laws of (5).   3. mortal sin   4. intention   5. fast
4. Knowingly to receive Communion while in mortal sin is a (6).   6. sacrilege
5. Drinking water does not break the (7).   7. fast

Problems for Discussion

1. John was a minute late for Mass on Sunday because his bus was late. May he go to Communion?

2. Mary ate a cookie at 7:30, before she came to school on First Friday. May she go to Communion at the 8:00 o'clock Mass? at the 11:30 Mass?

IV. ANSWERS TO STUDY EXERCISES FOR UNIT THREE, SECTION IV, PART THREE

(Textbook, pp. 286–287)

Completion (pp. 286–287)

1. Easter time
2. sacrilege
3. three hours
4. mortal sin
5. Pius XII
6. water
7. charity
8. sin
9. Holy Eucharist (H. E.)
10. fourth

SECTION V: Christ Restores or Increases the Life of Grace in Our Soul: Penance and Indulgences

(Text, pp. 291–354; Baltimore Catechism, Lessons 29–33)

OUTLINE OF UNIT III, SECTION V

A. **What the Sacrament of Penance Is** (Text, pp. 291–298)
1. Penance Was Instituted by Christ (Text, pp. 294–295)
2. Power to Forgive Sins Was Conferred on the Apostles and Their Successors (Text, pp. 295–297)
3. Sins Are Forgiven Through the Absolution of the Priest (Text, pp. 297–298)

B. **Penance Produces Wonderful Effects in the Soul** (Text, pp. 298–302)
1. Restores or Increases Sanctifying Grace (Text, p. 299)
2. Forgives Sins (Text, pp. 299–300)
3. Remits Punishment Due to Sins (Text, pp. 300–301)
4. Helps to Avoid Sin (Text, p. 301)
5. Restores Merits Lost by Mortal Sin (Text, p. 301)
6. Other Effects of the Sacrament of Penance (Text, p. 301)

C. **Acts Required for Worthy Reception of Penance** (Text, pp. 302–345)
1. Examine Our Conscience (Text, pp. 302–303)
2. Have Sorrow for Our Sins (Text, pp. 307–315)
   a) Sorrow Should Be Interior (Text, pp. 308–309)
   b) Sorrow Should Be Supernatural (Text, pp. 309–310)
   c) Sorrow Should Be Supreme (Text, p. 310)
   d) Sorrow Should Be Universal (Text, pp. 311–312)
3. Have the Firm Purpose of Not Sinning Again (Text, pp. 315–317)
4. Confess Our Sins to the Priest (Text, pp. 322–328)
5. Be Willing to Perform the Penance the Priest Gives Us (Text, pp. 328–332)

D. **Formula for Confession** (Text, pp. 335–339)

OUTLINE ON INDULGENCES

(Text, pp. 345–354; Lesson 33)

A. **Indulgences Are Short Cuts to Heaven** (Text, pp. 345–346)

B. **Indulgences Are of Two Kinds** (Text, pp. 346–347)

C. **Indulgences Remit Temporal Punishment** (Text, pp. 347–348)

D. **What We Can Do to Gain Indulgences** (Text, p. 348)

E. **Indulgences Greatly Help the Poor Souls** (Text, pp. 349–350)

F. **What Indulgences Really Mean** (Text, p. 350)

TEACHING SUGGESTIONS FOR UNIT THREE, SECTION V

I. OBJECTIVES

A. **Primary Objective**

To develop a deeper understanding and appreciation of the effects of the Sacrament of Penance.

B. **Auxiliary Objectives**

For the Intellect:
1. To develop in the children an increased knowledge and appreciation of the sacrament of Penance and its special sacramental grace.
2. To realize that all sin must be punished, for God is not only merciful but also just.
3. To find out how to make up for the temporal punishment due to sin.

For the Will:
1. To use the sacrament frequently and fervently.
2. To acquire the habit of saying the Act of Contrition each night.

II. NOTES ON TEACHER PRESENTATION

A. **Suggestions for Developing Understanding of Subject Matter**
1. View the filmstrip: *The Sacrament of Penance.*
2. Tell the story of the Prodigal Son. Get an appreciation of what sin does to us. Review the effects of sin — venial and mortal.
3. *Scripture Hunt:* Discuss the parable. Derive a lesson which we can practice in our daily living: Mt. 9:1–8; Jn. 20:19–23; Lk. 7:36–50; Lk. 23:39–43; Lk. 18:9–14; Mt. 7:24–27. Also find the essentials of confession in the above texts.
4. *Picture Study:* Derive the essentials for the sacrament of Penance and our application:

Christ and the Sinner   Mary Magdalen
The Good Thief   Crucifixion
The Good Shepherd   Denial of St. Peter
Peter, the Repentant   Christ, the Consoler

5. Discuss one of the case studies:

   a) John conceals a serious sin in confession by making it sound like a venial sin. What would you say about his confession?

   b) Ronald says that he finds it difficult to prepare for confession. Tell him why a daily examination of conscience will help him. Tell him how to make this examination.

   c) Geraldine says, "I am not sure that I have true contrition or sorrow for my sins because I never feel like crying." Explain to her what true contrition is.

6. Quote the words of Christ showing that He gave the Church the power to grant indulgences: Mt. 18:18; 16:13–19.

7. Discuss how indulgences may be used as a form of charity toward the souls in purgatory.

8. Explain why the following example is a good illustration of the doctrine of indulgences: Reginald comes to the rescue of his brother Justin who is heavily in debt. He pays his bills and thereby calls off his creditors.

9. *Quiz game:* Review the questions on penance and indulgences.

10. *Research:* How did the early Christians do penance for their sins? How are indulgences a substitute for long public penances practiced in the earlier ages of the Church?

B. Correlating Activities

1. Plan a bulletin-board display (with Scripture texts) illustrating scenes in which Christ forgave sins.

2. Have oral reports on the following parables. Show how our Lord during His lifetime used His power to forgive sins. What happens in each case? Lk. 7:36–50; Jn. 8:3–11; Lk. 23:39–43; Lk. 18:9–14; Mt. 22:36–40.

3. Dramatize a passage from the New Testament which presents Christ forgiving sins.

4. Conduct a panel discussion on "The Value of Confession," on "Christ's Attitude Toward Sinners."

5. Three people in the Gospel help us learn the true meaning of sorrow. *Read* the account of each and then *discuss* the real meaning of sorrow.

   a) Judas — Mt. 26:21–25; 27:1–5.

   b) Mary Magdalen — Lk. 7:36–50.

   c) St. Peter — Mk. 14:66–72.

6. Find stories in mission magazines of priests or people going long distances to administer or receive this sacrament.

7. Draw a picture of the interior of a bank with seven tellers' windows, labeling these respectively: Masses, Prayers, Sacraments, Indulgences, Sacramentals, Works of Mercy, Penances. Print the caption: *Spiritual Treasury Deposits.*

8. Tell the story of St. John Nepomucene's guarding the seal of the confessional.

9. Discuss our opportunities to help sinners by prayer and sacrifice. Suggest little acts of mortification that boys and girls can offer as penance.

10. Meditate on Christ's forgiving love and of our own lack of forgiveness, promising God that we will pardon others, and asking God to continue to love and pardon us.

11. Prepare a one-minute talk on one of the following topics:

    a) The Value of Confession

    b) Frequent Confession, a Preventive Measure and a Spiritual Vitamin.

    c) The Forgiveness of Sins, Another Proof of God's Merciful Love for Us.

    d) Confession Heals; Confession Justifies; Confession Grants Pardon

12. Memorize the "Prayer Before a Crucifix," said after Holy Communion.

13. Group discussion:

    a) Why contrition is the most important part of the sacrament of Penance.

    b) How daily examination of conscience helps one to lead a good life.

    c) Our privilege of receiving the sacrament of Penance frequently to obtain pardon and to restore or strengthen our supernatural life.

    d) Our opportunities to lessen the temporal punishment due to our sins by gaining indulgences.

14. List ten indulgenced ejaculations. Memorize a few (see *Raccolta*).

15. What advice would you give each of the following persons?

    a) A girl thinks she has not enough sins to confess so she adds other sins she did not commit.

    b) A boy rushes into the church, and finds no other penitents ahead of him. He hurries through his examination of conscience and then goes into the confessional.

    c) A boy believes that God alone can forgive sins. He cannot believe that a priest, who is a man like ourselves, can do so.

    d) A boy has a serious sin to confess, but he is very friendly with the priest, and is ashamed to tell him about it.

    e) John, a careless Catholic, has been away from the sacraments for eight months. He is making the confession for his Easter-duty Communion. In telling his sins he accuses himself this way: "I missed Mass lots of times; I ate meat on Friday a great number of times, etc."

16. *Discuss:* Why is this prayer of the leper, "If thou wilt, thou canst make me clean" (Mk. 1:40) a good one to use in preparing for confession?

17. What is your answer:
   a) Can Myron, who has just sinned grievously, gain an indulgence?
   b) Anne, one of the girls in your class, recites a prayer to which an indulgence of forty days is attached. Will her stay in purgatory be lessened forty days?
18. Mention some of the works enjoined for gaining a plenary indulgence.

C. Application

1. Be patient in disappointments and in bearing pain in reparation for sin.
2. Receive the sacrament of Penance with the greatest spiritual profit.
3. Get the habit of going to confession regularly, and at least once a month all during your life.
4. Receive the sacrament of Penance as soon as possible if unfortunately you have offended God in a serious way.
5. Keep in God's friendship by nightly examination of conscience followed by a sincere act of contrition.
6. Deprive yourself of something you enjoy as part payment of the temporal punishment due to your sins.
7. Say ejaculatory prayers during the day for the suffering souls in purgatory.

III. EVALUATION

Multiple Choice: Print the letter of your choice in the answer blank at the right.

1. The supernatural life of the soul is destroyed   1. D
by
   A. many venial sins   C. many imperfections
   B. serious temptations   D. a mortal sin

2. Sins are forgiven through the   2. D
   A. indulgences granted by the Church
   B. merits of saints
   C. merits of priests
   D. merits of Jesus Christ

3. The most important part of the sacrament of   3. C
Penance is
   A. examination of conscience   C. contrition
   B. confession   D. satisfaction

4. The best way to make an act of perfect con-   4. A
trition is by thinking about
   A. the great love of Jesus for us as shown by His death
   B. the happiness lost
   C. the punishment incurred
   D. the disgrace brought upon ourselves

5. We should go to confession   5. C
   A. to thank God for favors received
   B. to please our parents
   C. to obtain God's forgiveness and grace
   D. so that we can enjoy a good feeling

6. Christ gave the Apostles the power to forgive   6. A
sins
   A. on the evening of His resurrection
   B. on Pentecost
   C. before His ascension
   D. at the Last Supper

7. When a person is sorry for his sins because   7. B
they offend God, his sorrow is
   A. apostolic   C. universal
   B. supernatural   D. supreme

8. Choose the story that best portrays the   8. A
qualities of a good penitent:
   A. Mary Magdalen   C. Rich Young Man
   B. the Good Samaritan   D. the Centurion

9. The chief reason we are given a penance   9. B
is to
   A. resist temptation
   B. satisfy for the punishment due to our sins
   C. make ourselves strong
   D. imitate the saints

10. An indulgence is the   10. C
   A. remission of sin
   B. elimination of eternal punishment
   C. removal of temporal punishment for sin
   D. permission to commit sin

11. We cannot gain an indulgence for   11. A
   A. other living persons
   B. souls in purgatory
   C. ourselves
   D. anyone except the souls in purgatory

12. One must be in the state of grace to   12. D
   A. pray   C. make use of a sacramental
   B. attend Mass   D. gain an indulgence

13. An indulgence takes away   13. C
   A. grace   C. temporal punishment
   B. sin   D. eternal punishment

14. Full remission of the temporal punishment   14. C
due to sin is
   A. partial indulgence   C. plenary indulgence
   B. perfect contrition   D. sanctifying grace

IV. ANSWER TO STUDY EXERCISES FOR UNIT THREE, SECTION V

(Text, pp. 304–305; 317–318; 340–342; 351–352)

I. Completion (p. 304):
1. eternal
2. temporal
3. temporal
4. Jesus Christ
5. priest

II. Missing Words (p. 304):
1. (a) know; (b) confess
2. merits

52

3. examination of conscience
4. sanctifying grace
5. (a) forgive; (b) forgiven; (c) retain; (d) retained

I. Completion (pp. 317–318):

1. true (perfect)
2. sin
3. perfect
4. contrition
5. imperfect
6. heart
7. make an act of contrition (perfect)
8. contrition — examination of conscience
9. universal
10. sin

II. True — False (p. 318):

1. False	3. True	5. True	7. True	9. True
2. True	4. False	6. True	8. False	10. True

GENERAL TEST ON THE SACRAMENT OF PENANCE
(pp. 340–342)

I. Yes or No (pp. 340–341):

1. No	6. No	11. No	16. Yes	21. Yes
2. Yes	7. Yes	12. No	17. No	22. Yes
3. Yes	8. Yes	13. No	18. Yes	23. Yes
4. No	9. No	14. Yes	19. Yes	24. Yes
5. No	10. No	15. Yes	20. Yes	

II. Matching (p. 342):

1. C	3. J	5. B	7. A	9. I
2. E	4. G	6. H	8. F	10. D

III. Recognition (p. 342):

1. Ask God's help . . .
2. Examine . . .
3. Be sorry . . .
4. Have firm purpose . . .
5. Confess . . .
6. Be willing . . .

TEST ON INDULGENCES (pp. 351–352)

True — False:

1. False	3. True	5. False	7. True	9. True
2. True	4. True	6. False	8. True	10. True

SECTION VI: Christ Prepares the Soul for Eternity in the Sacrament of Extreme Unction
(Text, pp. 354–369; Baltimore Catechism, Lesson 34)

OUTLINE OF UNIT THREE, SECTION VI

A. **Extreme Unction Gives Health and Strength to the Soul and Sometimes to the Body** (Text, pp. 355–357)
B. **Extreme Unction Should Be Received by Those Who Are in Danger of Death From Sickness, Accident, or Old Age** (Text, pp. 357–358)
C. **The Effects of Extreme Unction** (Text, pp. 358–359)
D. **Extreme Unction in Certain Circumstances Takes Away Mortal Sin** (Text, p. 360)
E. **Extreme Unction Should Be Preceded by a Suitable Preparation** (Text, pp. 361–362)
F. **The Priest Is the Minister of the Sacrament of Extreme Unction** (Text, pp. 362–363)
G. **The Priest Should Be Asked to Visit the Sick in Any Serious Illness** (Text, p. 363)
H. **The Priest Should Be Called in Case of Sudden or Unexpected Death** (Text, 363–364)

TEACHING SUGGESTIONS FOR UNIT THREE SECTION VI

I. OBJECTIVES

A. **Primary Objective**

To understand why the Sacrament of Extreme Unction is so important.

B. **Auxiliary Objectives**

For the Intellect:

1. To realize the importance of the Sacrament of Extreme Unction.
2. To realize that Extreme Unction is a special gift of God's love.

For the Will:

To form a great desire to receive the Last Sacraments.

II. NOTES ON TEACHER PRESENTATION

A. **Suggestions for Developing Understanding of Subject Matter**

1. Read the story of Christ healing the sick man (Jn. 5:1–15) and the instruction of St. James (James 5:14–15). Christ loves His sick and the accounts given in the New Testament will interest the pupils and give them an appreciation for this sacrament.
2. *Problem for discussion:* Miss McCloyd became seriously sick in the night. "Call the doctor," Mrs. McCloyd cried to her husband. "Shall I call the priest?" Bob asked. "Wait," replied Mrs. McCloyd. The doctor told Mrs. McCloyd that her daughter might not recover. "She must be kept quiet," the doctor said. "That means," Mr. McCloyd said, "that we must not call the priest yet. We will wait." What would you say? What advice can you give?
3. *Picture study:* Picture of Christ healing the sick. Example: "Cure of Centurion's Servant." Discuss picture with the help of these questions: Who? What? When? How? Why? Picture illustrating the administering of Extreme Unction. Use the above questions.
4. From the words of St. James 5:14–15, deduce the teaching of the Church on the Sacrament of Extreme Unction:
   a) The outward sign
   b) Institution by Christ
   c) Minister
   d) Recipient
   e) The effects of the sacrament on the soul and the body

B. Correlating Activities

1. Write a paragraph on the following topic: "A Good Life Is a Preparation for a Happy Death."
2. Make a frieze, movie, or series of tableaux or panels illustrating Christ's helping the sick in body and soul.
3. Discuss:
   a) "A Catholic deathbed follows a good Catholic life."
   b) "A Catholic funeral gives the Catholic God's final blessing."
4. Find and be prepared to tell what Christ did and said in the following incidents: Mt. 8:14–15; Jn. 9:1–12; Mk. 7:32–35; Mt. 8:1–3; 9:1–7.
5. Prepare a floor talk on "The Benefits of Extreme Unction."
6. Have a committee set up a sick-call table for the Last Sacraments. Each member explains the use of one article.
7. Explain our Lord's last seven words when dying on the cross and apply each one to your own death.
8. Point out the different errors of judgment in the following cases:
   a) Mrs. Jordan's husband is dying. She insists on having the doctor administer morphine before the priest comes, although it would be possible for her husband to endure his pain.
   b) Mr. Zeller dies suddenly of heart failure. His family do not telephone for the priest, as it is evident that Mr. Zeller is already dead.
   c) Allan Zeke refuses to get a priest for his dying father because he is afraid it will disturb him and make him worse.
9. Your uncle has recently died. He had lived a good Catholic life. He died fortified by the rites of the Catholic Church. Your aunt is very grieved. Write her a letter of sympathy. SUGGESTION: Think over the truths you have learned in this unit. Which ones would be most consoling to her?
10. Compare the death of a Catholic with that of a non-Catholic.
11. Dramatize what to do if a person is in danger of death.
12. What is your answer:
   a) Myron is going to cross the ocean on an airliner. He feels that there is a great danger to his life in such a trip and wants to be anointed before he goes. Why will the priest have to refuse to give him the sacrament of Extreme Unction in his case?
   b) Seven Catholic girls go for a swim in a neighborhood pond. One of them, Marjorie, drowns. They recover her body one hour later, and immediately begin first-aid efforts to revive her. Joan goes to get a doctor.

Should Patricia bother about getting a priest? Why?
13. Compose a short prayer asking for the grace of a happy death.
14. Meditate on the goodness of God, as shown by the institution of the sacrament of Extreme Unction.

C. Application

1. Pray every day, particularly to St. Joseph, the patron of a happy death, that you will be granted the grace to receive the last sacraments when the hour of your death draws near.
2. Pray daily for those in their last agony.
3. Wear a medal or scapular, as evidence of Catholicity in case of accident.
4. Recite short ejaculatory prayers which will help the sick person to remain closely united with God.
5. Resolve to help everyone receive this sacrament when the need arises.
6. Be resigned to the will of God regarding the time and manner of your death.
7. Keep in mind always the account you must render in the Last Judgment.

III. EVALUATION

Multiple Choice: Print the letter of your choice in the answer blank at the right.

1. The sacrament which gives health and strength to the soul and sometimes to the body when we are in danger of death is   1. D
   A. Baptism   C. Holy Eucharist
   B. Confirmation   D. Extreme Unction

2. Holy Communion given to those who are in danger of death is called   2. A
   A. Viaticum
   B. Extreme Unction
   C. a spiritual work of mercy
   D. a fruit of the Holy Ghost

3. Extreme Unction   3. C
   A. never takes away mortal sin
   B. always has the primary purpose of giving physical comfort to the dying
   C. sometimes remits mortal sin
   D. never removes actual sin

4. Extreme Unction may be administered to   4. D
   A. a criminal before going to his death
   B. a baby
   C. a person who has never had the use of reason
   D. a person dying of old age

5. The sacrament of Extreme Unction should be administered   5. A
   A. as soon as a person is seriously ill
   B. after a person becomes unconscious
   C. after the person is dead
   D. whenever the baby is sick

Completion: Supply the missing word or words. Write the answers in the space on the right.

1. Extreme Unction is given only to those who have reached the use of (1).

    1. reason

2. The effects of the sacrament of Extreme Unction are: an (2) of sanctifying grace; comfort in (3), and strength against (4); preparation for entrance into (5) by the remission of our sins and the cleansing of our souls from the (6) of sin; (7) of the body when it is good for the soul.

    2. increase
    3. sickness
    4. temptation
    5. heaven
    6. remains
    7. health

3. We should prepare ourselves to receive the sacrament of Extreme Unction by acts of (8), (9), (10), and especially by (11) to the will of God.

    8. faith
    9. hope
    10. charity
    11. resignation

4. The articles needed for the sick-call table for the administration of the sacrament are: (12).

    12. table, white covering, crucifix, two candles, holy water, cotton, glass of water, spoon

IV. ANSWERS TO STUDY EXERCISES FOR UNIT THREE, SECTION VI
(Text, pp. 366–367)

I. Problems (p. 366):
1–6. Answers will vary.
4. Baptism, Confirmation, Extreme Unction

II. True or False (pp. 366–367):

1. False	3. True	5. False	7. True
2. False	4. True	6. True	

III. Matching (p. 367):

1. F	3. H	5. C	7. A
2. E	4. G	6. B	8. D

ANSWERS TO END OF UNIT TESTS FOR UNIT THREE, SECTIONS IV, V, VI (Text, pp. 369–373)

I. Multiple Choice (pp. 369–370)

1. D	4. D	7. D	10. A
2. C	5. B	8. A	11. D
3. C	6. C	9. C	

II. Completion (pp. 370–371):
1. Mass
2. (a) prayer (b) sacraments
3. sacrilege
4. Confession
5. contrition
6. eternal
7. (a) world (b) purgatory
8. seal
9. Last Supper
10. health
11. sin
12. dispositions
13. Transubstantiation
14. Christ
15. Holy Communion
16. (a) restores (b) increases
17. Holy Viaticum

III. Matching: Part I (p. 372):

1. G	3. H	5. I	7. B	9. C
2. F	4. A	6. D	8. J	10. E

IV. Matching: Part II (p. 373):

1. A	3. F	5. I	7. H	9. G
2. D	4. B	6. E	8. J	10. C

REFERENCES AND MATERIALS
UNIT THREE — LIVING THROUGH CHRIST WITH CHRIST, AND IN CHRIST

A. Pupil References

Baierl, Rev. Joseph A., S.T.D., *A Method of Confession and of Holy Communion* (Rochester, N. Y.: Seminary Press).

Bandas, Rev. Rudolph G., and School Sisters of Notre Dame, *The Vine and the Branches,* Highway to Heaven Series, Book V (Milwaukee: Bruce, 1942).

Croft, Aloysius, *Twenty-One Saints* (Milwaukee: Bruce, 1937).

Dennerle, Rev. George M., and Rath, Rev. John C., *I Receive the Holy Ghost* (St. Paul, Minn.: Catechetical Guild).

Dooley, Rev. Lester M., *Hello Halo* (New York: Lumen Press, 1942).

——— *I Accuse Myself* (Techny, Ill.: Mission Press, 1942).

Drees, Rev. Victor, *A Pictorial Explanation of the Seven Sacraments* (Cincinnati: St. Anthony Messenger, 1941).

Fulkerson, Benjamin R., S.J., *Tips on Temptation* (St. Louis: Queen's Work).

Gasparri, Peter Cardinal, *Catholic Faith, Book III* (New York: Kenedy).

Greenstock, David L., *Christopher's Talks to Catholic Children* (New York: Burns, Oates, 1939).

Justina, Sister, O.S.B., *The Sacraments in Symbols* (St. Paul: Catechetical Guild).

Kelly, Rev. William R., Goebel, Rev. Edmund J., Imelda, Sister Mary, and Dougherty, Rev. Daniel M., *Living in God's Church,* Living My Religion Series, Book VI (New York: Benziger, 1942).

Mannix, Mary E., *Illustrated Lives of Patron Saints for Boys* (New York: Benziger).

——— *Illustrated Lives of Patron Saints for Girls* (New York: Benziger).

McGuire, Rev. Michael A., *Baltimore Catechism No. II,* Official Revised Edition (New York: Benziger, 1942).

Pfeiffer, Rev. Harold A., *The Catholic Picture Dictionary* (New York: Catholic Manufacturing Company).

B. Teacher References

Aurelia, Sister M., and Kirsch, Felix M., *Practical Aids for Catholic Teachers* (New York: Benziger, 1928, 1935).

Baierl, Rev. J., *The Sacraments Explained* (Rochester: Seminary Press, 1934).

Bandas, Rudolph, *Practical Problems in Religion* (Milwaukee: Bruce, 1934).

Chisholm, Rev. D., *The Catechism in Examples*, Vol. IV (New York: Benziger).

D'Ales, A., S.J., *Baptism and Confirmation* (St. Louis: Herder).

Dennerle, Rev. George M., "Preparing Children for Confession," *Catholic School Journal*, XXXV, May, 1935, pp. 111–114.

Devine, A., *The Sacraments Explained* (New York: Benziger, 1942).

Dooley, Rev., *The Holy Ghost — God of Love* (New York: Paulist Press) (pamphlet).

Dougherty, Rev. D. M., *Confirmation for Children* (New York: Paulist Press) (pamphlet).

Doyle, F., *The Wonderful Sacraments* (New York: Benziger).

Drinkwater, Rev. F. H., *Teaching the Catechism, Part III* (London: Burns, Oates, and Washbourne, 1936).

Ellard, G., S.J., *Christian Life and Worship* (Milwaukee: Bruce, 1940).

Goodier, A., *Saints for Sinners* (New York: Sheed & Ward, 1943).

Hagan, Rt. Rev. Msgr. John, *A Compendium of Catechetical Instruction*, Vol. II: *The Sacraments* (New York: Benziger, 1928).

Harrington, H., *The Sacrament of Penance* (New York: Macmillan).

Howell, O., *Sacraments and Sacrifice* (Collegeville, Minn.: Liturgical Press, 1952).

Husslein, J., *Heroines of Christ* (Milwaukee: Bruce, 1939).

Kelly, B., *The Sacraments of Daily Living* (New York: Sheed & Ward).

Kelly, Rev. William, *Our Sacraments* (New York: Benziger).

Kilker, A., *Extreme Unction* (St. Louis: Herder).

Kinkead, T., *Explanation of the Baltimore Catechism* (New York: Benziger).

Kolbe, F., *The Sacrament of Confirmation* (New York: Macmillan).

Louvel, Putz, *Signs of Faith* (Chicago: Fides, 1953).

Marmion, Rt. Rev. D. Columba, *Christ the Life of the Soul* (St. Louis: Herder, 1939).

McNeil and Aaron, *Means of Grace* (Paterson, N. J.: St. Anthony Guild).

O'Brien, Rev. John A., *Understanding the Faith*, Official Revision of *Baltimore Catechism No. 3* (Notre Dame, Ind.: Ave Maria Press).

O'Connor, Jerome F., and Hayden, William, *Chalk Talks*, or *Teaching Catechism Graphically*, Four Parts, third edition (St. Louis: The Queen's Work, 1937).

O'Rafferty, *Instructions on Christian Doctrine* (Milwaukee: Bruce).

Palmer, Paul, S.J., *Sacraments and Worship* (Westminster, Md.: Newman, 1954).

Plus, Raoul, S.J., *Baptism and Confirmation* (London: Burns, Oates, & Washbourne).

Quinlan, Rev. Patrick, *The Powerful Sacraments* (Chicago: Loyola University Press).

Ryan, *The Sacramental Way* (New York: Sheed & Ward, 1948).

Schumacher, Rt. Rev. Msgr. M. A., *How to Teach the Catechism, Vol. III* (New York: Benziger, 1946).

Sheerin, Paul, C.S.P., *The Sacrament of Freedom* (Milwaukee: Bruce, 1961).

Spirago-Clarke, *The Catechism Explained* (New York: Benziger).

Strasser, Bernard, *With Christ Through the Year* (Milwaukee: Bruce, 1957).

Sullivan, J., *Fundamentals of Catholic Belief* (New York: Kenedy).

Urban, A., *Teacher's Handbook of the Christian Religion* (New York: Benziger).

C. Materials (Audio-Visual Aids)

SLIDES:

Fr. Lehane's Set: all sacraments

SYMBOLS:

The Sacraments in Symbols — 7 charts, Catechetical Guild, St. Paul, Minn.

The Eucharist in Symbols — 23 symbols, Catechetical Guild, St. Paul, Minn.

The Church Year in Symbols, Catechetical Guild, St. Paul Minn.

FILMSTRIP:

The Sacraments, Society for Visual Education, Chicago, Ill.

The Sacraments, St. John University

UNIT FOUR. CHRIST WORKS THROUGH US

(Text, pp. 374–413)

OUTLINE OF CONTENT

I. Vocations in General — Christ Has Work for Each of Us to Do
(Text, pp. 379–384)

II. The Priesthood: The Sacrament of Holy Orders — Christ Acts in and Through His Priests
(Text, pp. 385–396; Baltimore Catechism, Lesson 34)

III. The Married State: The Sacrament of Matrimony — Christ Works Through Married People
(Text, pp. 397–413; Baltimore Catechism, Lesson 35)

SECTION I: Vocations in General — Christ Has Work for Each of Us to Do

(Text, pp. 379–384)

SECTION II: The Priesthood: The Sacrament of Holy Orders — Christ Acts in and Through His Priests

(Text, pp. 385–396; Baltimore Catechism, Lesson 34)

OUTLINE OF UNIT FOUR, SECTION I

A. What a Vocation Is (Text, p. 379)

B. There Are Three Definite Types of Vocations (Text, pp. 379–382)

C. Certain Qualifications Are Required for Each State (Text, pp. 382–384)

OUTLINE OF UNIT FOUR, SECTION II

A. Christ Acts in and Through His Priests (Text, pp. 385–386)

B. The Requirements for Admission to the Priesthood (Text, pp. 386–387)

C. The Steps That Lead to the Priesthood (Text, p. 387)

D. The Effects of the Sacrament of Holy Orders (Text, pp. 387–392)

E. What Our Attitude Toward the Priest Should Be (Text, pp. 392–393)

TEACHING SUGGESTIONS FOR UNIT IV, SECTIONS I, II

I. OBJECTIVES

A. Primary Objective

To understand how God uses human instruments, weakened by original sin but strengthened by sanctifying grace, to further His work, and to pray often that God's will be carried out with regard to vocations.

B. Auxiliary Objectives

For the Intellect:

1. To understand that the priest is another Christ and as such merits our honor and respect.
2. To appreciate the great dignity of the priesthood.
3. To realize that marriage is a holy state of life and is according to God's plan.
4. To know that certain conditions are required for the reception of Holy Orders or Matrimony.

For the Will:

1. To co-operate with the priest in carrying out Christ's work of saving souls.
2. To show respect to every priest because He represents Christ.
3. To pray that God may direct us in our choice of vocations.
4. To resolve to obey the regulations of the Church and the State with regard to marriage.

II. NOTES ON TEACHER PRESENTATION

A. Suggestions for Developing Understanding of Subject Matter

1. Draw on the board a picture of an altar and on the seven steps leading to it, print the names of the four minor orders and the three major orders.
2. Have the class examine Scripture for references concerning the priesthood.
3. Conduct a question-box period. Everyone may

ask one or two questions on Holy Orders which will be answered by a selected group from the class.

B. Correlating Activities

1. Write a paragraph explaining to a Protestant why we honor our priests.
2. Enumerate the different blessings of religion that you may receive from priests.
3. If you were asked to make up a quiz on Holy Orders, what points would you include?
4. Imagine you are a freshman. Your religion teacher asks you to defend this statement: "It is impossible to carry on the work of the Church without priests." Can you do it?
5. Formulate a list of twelve to fifteen terms regarding the priesthood, and see how many in your class can define them correctly (major orders, tonsure, sacred ministry, etc.).
6. Using the outline given, prepare a talk on Holy Orders.

C. Application

1. Encourage prayers for priests.
2. Teach reverence for priests as representatives of Christ and to show how we can help them in every possible way.
3. Aid children in acquiring the habit of praying to know God's will and to ask for courage to follow it. "Teach me, O Lord, to do Thy will, for Thou art my God" (500 days' indulgence).

III. EVALUATION

Completion: Number your paper from 1 to 10. After the number write the word or words needed to complete the sentence.

1. The chief supernatural powers of the priests are (1) and (2).

   1. to change bread and wine into the body and blood of Christ in the Holy Sacrifice of the Mass
   2. to forgive sins in the sacrament of Penance

2. The (3) is the minister of the sacrament of Holy Orders
   3. bishop
3. The (4) is the highest of the major orders.
   4. priesthood
4. To become a priest one must ordinarily be (5) years of age.
   5. 24 years
5. A (6) is the place in which men prepare for the priesthood.
   6. seminary
6. The grace through which the priest has God's constant help in his sacred ministry is called (7).
   7. sacramental

7. The priest is the representative of (8).
   8. Christ
8. It is the (9) who receives the fullness of the priesthood.
   9. bishop
9. The highest motive for entering the priesthood would be (10).
   10. honor and glory of God

Essay: Write a paper of about one hundred to one hundred and fifty words on one of the following:

1. The growth and protection of a vocation from childhood to ordination day.
2. What we owe to the priesthood.

IV. ANSWERS TO STUDY EXERCISE FOR UNIT FOUR, SECTION II

(Text, p. 394)

Multiple Choice (p. 394):

1. B	3. A	5. A	7. A	9. C
2. A	4. A	6. B	8. A	10. B

SECTION III: Christ Works Through Married People

(Text, pp. 397–413; Baltimore Catechism, Lesson 35)

OUTLINE OF UNIT FOUR, SECTION III

A. What Matrimony Is (Text, pp. 397–399)

B. The Duties of Matrimony (Text, pp. 399–400)

C. Qualities of Christian Marriage (Text, pp. 400–402)

D. Marriage Is Sacred (Text, pp. 402–403)

E. Laws in General Governing Marriage (Text, pp. 403–404)

F. Two Kinds of Preparation Are Required (Text, pp. 404–406)
   1. Remote Preparation (Text, pp. 404–405)
   2. Immediate Preparation (Text, pp. 405–406)

G. The Effects of the Sacrament (Text, p. 406)

H. Christ's Blessing on the Marriage (Text, pp. 406–407)

TEACHING SUGGESTIONS FOR UNIT IV, SECTION III

I. OBJECTIVES

A. Primary Objective

To understand that the prime purpose of marriage is to share life and love with another (one's spouse) in order to give life and love to others (children).

B. Auxiliary Objectives

1. To engender a deep respect for the holiness of matrimony.
2. To develop good attitudes toward marriage.
3. To promote proper preparation for marriage — physical and economic as well as mental and spiritual.

II. NOTES ON TEACHER PRESENTATION

A. Suggestions for Developing Understanding of Subject Matter

1. List some of the Church's regulations regarding the marriage of baptized persons.
2. List the regulations made by the State concerning marriage as a contract.
3. Discuss why both the Church and the State are so vitally concerned with marriage.
4. Find in the New Testament the account of the marriage at Cana. What is one important lesson that people contemplating marriage could well take from this story?
5. Tabulate the qualities that would make a man or a woman a good partner in marriage.
6. Collect pictures about families from papers or magazines.
7. Write a paragraph about "My Favorite Family." Read it to the class and note in what ways families are similar.

B. Correlating Activities

1. God made marriage to last as long as husband and wife both live. What quotation did Christ give in reference to this?
2. What programs have you heard concerning family life? In how many can you find application of Christian social principles?
3. List any quotation or story concerning marriage from the New Testament.
4. By means of a chart, compare the Church's laws on marriage with the State's laws.
5. Compose a prayer to our Blessed Lady asking her guidance in the choice of a state of life.
6. Dramatize the story of the marriage at Cana.
7. Analyze recent movies you have seen and indicate which have contained wrong ideas about marriage, e.g., divorce.

C. Application

1. Increase our love and reverence for our parents.
2. Recite often the prayer to know one's state of life.
3. Understand that parents grow in grace as they fulfill their duties as Catholic parents.
4. Appreciate the fact that it is the obligation of everyone in the family to make it a truly holy family.

III. EVALUATION

Completion: Number your paper from 1 to 10. After a number write the word or words needed to complete the statement.

1. The official and necessary witness of the sacrament of Matrimony is the (1).   1. priest
2. Marriage is always a (2) when entered into by baptized persons.   2. sacrament
3. The Christian man and the Christian woman who make the marriage contract are the (3) of the sacrament of Matrimony.   3. ministers
4. Catholics who attempt marriage before a justice of the peace or before a non-Catholic minister contract an (4) marriage.   4. invalid
5. Parents must provide for the (5) welfare of their children as well as the (6) welfare.   5. spiritual
6. material
6. The bond of Christian marriage is broken only by (7).   7. death
7. The model of a Christian family is the (8).   8. Holy Family
8. The State has authority regarding only the (9) effects of marriage.   9. civil
9. In selecting a partner for life, (10) values should come first.   10. spiritual
10. The training of children is an obligation of the (11).   11. parents

ESSAY

How well can you write on one of the following?
1. The Catholic Church by defending marriages defends society.
2. Reasons why the Catholic Church discourages mixed marriages.
3. Ways in which the Christian wife and mother can be a real lay apostle.

IV. ANSWERS TO STUDY EXERCISES FOR UNIT FOUR, SECTION III

(Text, pp. 408—409)

I. Completion (p. 408):

1. religious
2. (a) priest and (b) two witnesses
3. Matrimony
4. Nuptial Mass
5. sacred
6. marry
7. (a) parents; (b) God
8. man and woman
9. (a) sacrament; (b) contract
10. (a) parents; (b) confessor

II. True — False (p. 409):

1. False 3. True 5. True 7. False 9. True
2. True 4. True 6. False 8. True 10. False

AN ADDITIONAL ACHIEVEMENT TEST FOR UNIT FOUR, SECTIONS I, II, III

Multiple Choice: Choose the correct answer and print the letter of your choice in the answer space on the right.

1. The minister of the Sacrament of Matrimony   1. B
   A. attendant   C. bishop
   B. bride and groom   D. priest

2. The Church forbids mixed marriages chiefly because   2. B
   A. they give the children improper training

B. they are often the source of spiritual dangers

C. they lead to family discord

D. they are not a fruitful source always of vocations

3. Jean and John have been married by the priest. Jean thinks that she has made a wrong choice and wants to marry Larry who is still single. She may not marry Larry until

A. permission is given

B. John says she may remarry

C. a divorce is granted

D. John dies

3. D

4. The marriage bond can be broken by

A. the private agreement of husband and wife

B. the permission of the Church to live separately

C. a civil divorce

D. the death of either party

4. D

5. A Catholic who goes to a justice of the peace or a minister to be married to a non-Catholic is

A. not married at all and commits a venial sin

B. married and commits no sin

C. not married at all and commits a grievous sin

D. really married although he commits a mortal sin

5. C

6. The sacrament of Matrimony gives grace to the bridal couple

A. for their whole married life

6. A

B. only for the day on which they are married

C. until they commit a mortal sin

7. The fact that marriage cannot be dissolved by any human power can be proved by the quotation:

A. "If you love me, keep the Commandments"

B. "Do this in remembrance of me"

C. "What therefore God has joined together, let no man put asunder"

D. "If any man will come after me, let him deny himself and take up his cross and follow me"

7. C

8. Holy Orders was instituted by Christ

A. on Holy Thursday

B. on Calvary

C. at the Ascension

8. A

9. The priest commands our reverence and respect *chiefly* because he

A. gives absolution in the sacrament of Penance

B. is a learned man

C. is appointed by the bishop

D. represents the priesthood of Christ

9. D

10. The priest fulfills his office of mediator between God and man by

A. fasting and abstaining on the days appointed

B. offering the Holy Sacrifice of the Mass

C. studying in the seminary

D. reading spiritual books

10. B

For bibliography, see the works listed on p. 55.

UNIT FIVE.   SANCTIFICATION THROUGH THE SACRAMENTALS AND PRAYER

(Text, pp. 414–461)

OUTLINE OF CONTENT

I. Sacramentals Obtain for Us From God Spiritual and Temporal Favors
(Text, pp. 419–430; Baltimore Catechism, Lesson 36)

II. Prayer Is Another Means of Obtaining God's Grace
(Text, pp. 431–446; Baltimore Catechism, Lesson 37)

III. The Our Father
(Text, pp. 447–461, Baltimore Catechism, Lesson 38)

SECTION I: Sacramentals Obtain for Us From God Spiritual and Temporal Favors

(Text, pp. 419–430; Baltimore Catechism, Lesson 36)

OUTLINE OF UNIT FIVE, SECTION I

A. Sacramentals Obtain Favors From God in Two Ways
(Text, pp. 419–421)
1. Through the Prayers of the Church Offered for Those Who Use Them (Text, pp. 419–420)
2. Through the Devotion They Inspire (Text, pp. 420–421)

B. Sacramentals Bestow Many Benefits (Text, pp. 421–424)
1. Actual Graces (Text, pp. 421–422)
2. The Forgiveness of Venial Sins; the Remission of Temporal Punishment (Text, p. 422)
3. Health of Body and Material Blessings (Text, pp. 422–424)
4. Protection From Evil Spirits (Text, p. 424)

C. Sacramentals Are of Various Kinds (Text, pp. 424–425)

D. Sacramentals Should Be Used With Faith and Devotion (Text, pp. 425–426)

TEACHING SUGGESTIONS FOR UNIT V, SECTION I

I. OBJECTIVES

A. Primary Objective
1. To learn the importance of prayer and the sacramentals as means of attaining sanctification.
2. To develop the will to use them.

B. Auxiliary Objectives

For the Intellect:
1. To learn what sacramentals are, the chief kinds, their source and purpose.
2. To learn the value and power of prayer.
3. To understand that prayer is a means of life and growth in supernatural living.
4. To learn the various kinds and levels of prayer.

For the Will:
1. To acquire the habit of making frequent use of sacramentals.
2. To make sure to use them with faith and devotion.
3. To appreciate the great privilege that is ours to speak with God in prayer.
4. To develop a life pattern of daily prayers.
5. To foster the habit of praying with humility, attention, and confidence.
6. To form the practice of saying indulgenced prayers frequently during the day, especially in time of temptation.
7. To be faithful in saying daily morning and night prayers.
8. To pray often the most perfect prayer, the Our Father.
9. To try to learn to use the higher forms of prayer.

II. NOTES ON TEACHER PRESENTATION

A. Suggestions for Developing Understanding of Subject Matter

1. "Father John was here today," Mrs. Stone said to her non-Catholic husband. "He blessed our home." "What does that mean?" Mr. Stone

asked. "Is that something new?" How would you explain this to Mr. Stone?

2. Have the prayer for the blessing of homes read, and instruct the pupils to note the blessings mentioned in the prayer.

3. On Ash Wednesday the priest places ashes on our foreheads and says these words: "Remember man that thou art dust and unto dust thou shalt return." Explain the source and meaning of this quotation.

4. Explain the reason we have our throats blessed on the feast of St. Blaise. Read the prayer that accompanies the blessing.

5. For class discussion:
   a) Things which I have seen today which make me think of God.
   b) Special value God has given to some of His creatures, for example: bread, water, wine, and oil.
   c) Instances which show how the earth in general and some particular creatures were sanctified by Christ. *Examples:* Man born blind — clay and water; Christ's garment cures woman.

6. Show filmstrips on sacramentals, if available.

7. Have a bulletin-board display of pictures of sacramentals.

8. Question the pupils about the sacramentals in use by them and in their homes.

B. Correlating Activities

1. Be prepared to report on blessings given by our Lord on certain occasions. Look up the following references: Mk. 10:16; Lk. 24:51.

2. Read to the class the translation of certain blessings of the Church. Refer to *Book of Friendliness* (Ginn).

3. Write a brief paragraph explaining the benefits obtained by the use of sacramentals.

4. Arrange a bulletin-board display of sacramentals, with simple explanations.

5. Start a campaign in your classroom encouraging the use of holy water and other sacramentals in the home. Draw posters to help vitalize the campaign.

6. Review the lesson on sacramentals.

7. Read the blessing for an automobile. What blessing is asked?

8. Report on the indulgences attached to the use of certain sacramentals.

9. Make a booklet of sacramentals containing illustrations and descriptions.

10. Dramatize a scene in which a non-Catholic asks and receives information about some common sacramentals.

11. Draw pictures of:
    a) A priest blessing little children
    b) A priest placing ashes on foreheads of children

12. Write a letter to a non-Catholic friend telling why good Catholics usually carry a rosary with them.

13. Make a list of sacramentals found in your home; in your school.

C. Application

1. Use every creature in such a way that it will become for us a "sacramental," leading us to God and His grace.

2. Remember always that the entire value of sacramentals depends upon our using them as the Church intends.

3. Find in the beauty of nature a faint reflection of the beauty of God.

4. Be grateful to God for the sacramentals which are a manifestation of His love for us.

III. EVALUATION

Multiple Choice: Choose the best answer or the only correct answer and print the letter of your choice in the answer space at the right.

1. Sacramentals   1. C
   A. give sanctifying grace   C. stir up devotion
   B. insure salvation   D. perform miracles

2. Holy things or acts set apart and blessed   2. B
   by the Church are
   A. mysteries   C. sacraments
   B. sacramentals

3. The following is a sacramental   3. B
   A. Holy Eucharist   C. Holy Orders
   B. holy water

4. Candles are blessed on   4. C
   A. Holy Saturday
   B. Pentecost
   C. February 2
   D. Immaculate Conception, December 8

5. The best way to give honor to the Blessed   5. A
   Virgin is to
   A. imitate her holy life   C. say the rosary
   B. make a May altar   D. wear her medal

6. All of the following are sacramentals except 6. D
   A. blessed ashes
   B. blessing of an automobile
   C. rosary
   D. blow on the cheek at Confirmation

Answer *yes* or *no to* the following questions:

1. Through the use of sacramentals we obtain   1. Yes
   the remission of temporal punishment.

2. The use of medals and scapulars is a super- 2. No
   stitious practice.

3. The sacramentals were instituted by Christ. 3. No

4. Sacramentals obtain grace from God   4. Yes
   through the devotion they inspire.

5. You will never be in an automobile accident if you wear a scapular.   5. No

6. We should use sacramentals with faith and devotion.   6. Yes

7. The blessing of a home is a sacramental.   7. Yes

8. Is their any similarity between Catholic veneration of images of our Lord or the saints and the devotion of the American people to historical pictures and statues?   8. Yes

9. The effectiveness of the grace of the sacramentals depends chiefly on the prayer of the Church.   9. Yes

10. A blessed crucifix is a sacramental.   10. Yes

IV. ANSWERS TO STUDY EXERCISES FOR UNIT FIVE, SECTION I

(Text, pp. 427–428)

I. True — False (p. 427):

1. True	3. False	5. False	7. True
2. False	4. True	6. True	8. False

II. Matching (p. 428):

1. C   2. F   3. A   4. E   5. D   6. B

SECTION II: Prayer Is Another Means of Obtaining God's Grace

(Text, pp. 431–446); Baltimore Catechism, Lesson 37)

SECTION III: The Our Father

(Text, pp. 447–460; Baltimore Catechism, Lesson 38)

OUTLINE OF UNIT FIVE, SECTION II

A. What Prayer Is (Text, pp. 431–432)

B. Prayer Has Various Purposes (Text, pp. 433–434)

C. Prayer Requires Certain Dispositions on Our Part (Text, pp. 434–442)

1. We Should Pray With Attention (Text, pp. 434–435)

2. We Should Pray With a Conviction of Our Own Helplessness and Our Dependence Upon God (Text, p. 435)

3. We Should Pray With a Great Desire for the Graces We Beg of Him (Text, pp. 435–436)

4. We Should Pray With Loving Trust in His Goodness (Text, p. 436)

5. We Should Pray With Perseverance (Text, pp. 436–437)

6. Our Prayer Should Be All-Inclusive (Text, p. 437)

7. Prayer Is Very Powerful (Text, pp. 437–439)

8. The Two Kinds of Prayer (Text, pp. 439–441)

9. There Are Prayers Every Catholic Should Know by Heart (Text, pp. 440–442)

OUTLINE OF UNIT FIVE, SECTION III

A. Introduction: Our Father Who Art in Heaven (Text, p. 448)

B. Seven Petitions (Text, pp. 449–457)

1. Hallowed Be Thy Name (Text, pp. 449–450)
2. Thy Kingdom Come (Text, p. 450)
3. Thy Will Be Done on Earth as It Is in Heaven (Text, p. 451)
4. Give Us This Day Our Daily Bread (Text, pp. 451–453)
5. And Forgive Us Our Trespasses as We Forgive Those Who Trespass Against Us (Text, pp. 453–455)
6. And Lead Us Not Into Temptation (Text, pp. 455–456)
7. But Deliver Us From Evil (Text, pp. 456–457)

C. Conclusion (Text, p. 457)

TEACHING SUGGESTIONS FOR UNIT V, SECTIONS II, III

I. OBJECTIVES

A. Primary Objective

To see why this prayer, given us by Jesus Himself, is so wonderful.

B. Auxiliary Objectives

For the Intellect:

1. To understand the nature of prayer.
2. To learn the purposes of prayer.
3. To learn the conditions for prayer.
4. To understand the kinds of prayer.
5. To analyze the Our Father.

For the Will:

1. To encourage the habit of prayer.
2. To develop attention and devotion during prayer.
3. To encourage life resolutions as regards prayer.

II. NOTES ON TEACHER PRESENTATION

A. Suggestions for Developing Understanding of Subject Matter

1. Select from the Gospels several examples of the efficacy of prayer, e.g., Mt. 7:7–11; 5:5–15. Report to the class.

2. To test understanding of catechism answers:
   a) What do we do when we adore God?
   b) Why do we thank God?
   c) What is meant by praying with perseverance?
   d) When are our distractions in prayer displeasing to God?
   e) Give a reason why our prayers are not always answered.
   f) What acts should every Catholic know by heart?

3. Panel discussion on the subject "Prayer Brings Us Grace" telling:
   a) What our Lord did about prayer on different occasions during His life.
   b) What He said about prayer.
   c) What resolutions we should make about prayer.

4. What does this statement mean? Our asking is the condition for our receiving.

5. What does the parable about the Pharisee and the Publican suggest to us about our own prayer?

6. Put on the blackboard the following word arrangement:

PRAYER $\begin{cases} \text{Thinking about God} \\ \text{Talking to God} \end{cases}$ with loving attention

Leave it there until you have developed the two kinds of prayer.

7. There is a big difference between "reading or saying prayers" and praying. Explain what is meant.

8. Explain why the Our Father is a prayer of perfect and unselfish love.

9. Read Lk. 11:1–4 which tells the story of the occasion when the disciples asked our Lord to teach them to pray. Have the pupils note how all the elements of prayer — adoration, thanksgiving, petition, atonement are found in the prayer He taught them — the Our Father.

10. Show how the petitions of the Our Father cover all our needs of soul and body.

11. To penetrate the meaning of catechism answers:
   a) Whom do we address as "Our Father" when we say the Lord's Prayer?
   b) Why do we say "our" and not "my" Father?
   c) Why do we say "this day" and "daily"?
   d) What do we mean by "trespasses"?
   e) Does God ever positively lead us into temptation?

12. Read to the class the lesson on prayer in Jn. 17, in which Jesus prays for Himself, for His disciples, and for His Church. Read Mt. 26:36–46 telling about His prayer during His night of agony on the Mount of Olives. What lessons can we learn about prayer from these scriptural passages?

13. Have a question box containing prayers that should be known by heart. Form teams to stimulate competition and hear their prayers.

14. Recite some of the Psalms — as our prayer to God; Christ's prayer for us.

B. Correlating Activities

1. Compose a prayer asking that you may find the joyousness in life which St. Francis of Assisi did.

2. All liturgical prayer is directed in the first place to the praise and glory of God, and second to the obtaining of graces and blessings. Show how this is true in the following prayers: the Our Father; the Preface; the *Gloria*.

3. Write a brief essay entitled "How I Can Pray Always."

4. Write the names of at least three persons whom you should remember in prayer every day. Tell why.

5. List two or more intentions for which you should pray daily; for example: grace of a happy death.

6. Review the catechism lesson on prayer.

7. Explain the meaning of the slogan: "The Family That Prays Together Stays Together."

8. Make a poster of the parish church. Use as caption: "My House Is a House of Prayer."

9. Look up and report to the class on stories of remarkable conversions and other effects of prayer.

10. Work out a simple plan for using passages from Sacred Scripture and other selections for mental prayer.

11. Make a report on the origin of the Hail Mary.

12. Find a prayer that can be used in praying for the welfare of our country (e.g., Bishop Carroll's). Read it to the class.

13. Make a poster illustrating persons praying together under various circumstances. Use suitable captions.

14. Help the class to draw up a list of intentions for individual or class prayer (e.g., pray for people in a certain persecuted country).

15. Tell in what part of the Lord's Prayer we ask:
   a) For all the things that are necessary to live
   b) To have our sins forgiven

16. Be prepared to recite the part of the Our Father which is in praise of God.

17. Write a paragraph telling why the "Our Father" is a perfect prayer.

18. Show how the following prayers follow the same form — first praise and then petition: the Our Father, the Hail Mary, the Memorare.

19. Review the catechism lesson on the Our Father.

20. Make a poster illustrating one or more of the petitions in the Our Father.

C. Application

1. Pray in your own words.

2. Practice simple meditation.

3. Take part in group prayer with the family, the class, the parish.

4. Maintain the habit of praying for our family and various persons.

5. Acquire the habit of offering the day for specific intentions.

6. Make frequent use of both mental and vocal prayer.

7. Thank God for a "good time" or any joy that comes to us.

8. Be faithful in saying morning and night prayers.

9. Pray for God's children throughout the world who do not know Him as we do

10. Meditate slowly and thoughtfully on the unselfish desires expressed in the Our Father.

11. Always include the Our Father in morning and night prayers.

III. EVALUATION

Multiple Choice: Choose the best answer or the only correct answer and print the letter of your choice in the space at the right.

1. Christ said we should pray   1. C
   - A. sometimes
   - B. in sickness
   - C. always
   - D. on Sunday

2. The most necessary prayer is   2. B
   - A. the Morning Offertory
   - B. the Act of Contrition
   - C. grace before meals
   - D. the Hail Mary

3. The prayer which was partly composed by   3. D an angel is the
   - A. Hail Holy Queen
   - B. Apostles' Creed
   - C. Memorare
   - D. Hail Mary

4. The most necessary requirement for prayer is   4. C
   - A. attention
   - B. the position
   - C. the intention
   - D. name of prayer

5. Prayers said with willful distractions   5. A
   - A. are displeasing to God
   - B. please God in a slight degree
   - C. gain some merit
   - D. add to God's honor

6. The prayer of the Publican exemplifies the   6. B virtue of
   - A. perseverance
   - B. humility
   - C. charity
   - D. meekness

7. Singing sacred hymns is an illustration of   7. D
   - A. mental prayer
   - B. contemplation
   - C. meditation
   - D. vocal prayer

8. A prayer which expresses a petition for a   8. A happy death
   - A. Hail Mary
   - B. Our Father
   - C. Act of Contrition
   - D. Apostles' Creed

9. Reverence for God's name is given special   9. D mention in the
   - A. Hail Mary
   - B. Confiteor
   - C. Apostles' Creed
   - D. Our Father

10. The prayer which especially commemorates   10. B the Annunciation is the
    - A. Morning Offering
    - B. Angelus
    - C. Apostles' Creed
    - D. Our Father

11. The sign of the cross expresses the mystery   11. B of the
    - A. Incarnation
    - B. Trinity
    - C. Ascension
    - D. Assumption

12. The best prayer is the   12. C
    - A. Hail Mary
    - B. Apostles' Creed
    - C. Our Father
    - D. Confiteor

13. The greatest of all prayers in the Mass is the   13. A
    - A. Pater Noster
    - B. Gloria
    - C. Kyrie
    - D. Agnus Dei

14. The *Pater Noster*   14. B
    - A. was introduced into the Mass by Christ
    - B. is the table prayer of God's children
    - C. is an act of contrition
    - D. introduces the Mass of the Faithful

15. Christ gave the Our Father to   15. D
    - A. the Holy Women
    - B. the Pharisees
    - C. St. Joseph
    - D. the Apostles

16. The number of petitions in the Our Father is   16. A
    - A. seven   B. two   C. ten   D. five

17. In the Our Father we pray that God may be   17. A known and honored by all men when we say
    - A. Thy kingdom come
    - B. hallowed be Thy name
    - C. deliver us from evil
    - D. Thy will be done on earth as it is in heaven

18. When we say the Lord's Prayer, we address   18. A as "Our Father" the
    - A. first person of the Blessed Trinity, God
    - B. second person of the Blessed Trinity, Jesus Christ
    - C. third person of the Blessed Trinity, the Holy Ghost
    - D. three Divine Persons of the Blessed Trinity

Problems and Exercises:

1. The sign of the cross is a symbol of our redemption through Christ. Explain the meaning of this statement.
2. Write the words of Our Lord's promise concerning prayer.
3. The church is the most fitting place in which to pray.
4. Which do you find hardest to say: morning prayers, grace before meals, night prayers? Why?
5. Tell in your own words the chief thoughts which arise in connection with the following words or phrases of the "Our Father."

OUR . . . _____

FATHER . . . _____

WHO ART IN HEAVEN . . . _____

HALLOWED BE THY NAME . . . _____

THY KINGDOM COME . . . _____

THY WILL BE DONE ON EARTH AS IT IS IN HEAVEN . . . _____

GIVE US THIS DAY OUR DAILY BREAD . . . _____

AND FORGIVE US OUR TRESPASSES AS WE FORGIVE THOSE WHO TRESPASS AGAINST US . . . _____

AND LEAD US NOT INTO TEMPTATION . . . _____

BUT DELIVER US FROM EVIL . . . _____

IV. ANSWERS TO STUDY EXERCISES FOR UNIT FIVE, SECTIONS II, III

(Text, pp. 443–444, 458)

I. Completion (p. 443):

1. loyalty
2. thank
3. pardon
4. ask
5. willful
6. words
7. (a) Blessed Trinity; (b) Redemption
8. (a) minds; (b) hearts

II. True — False (p. 443):

1. True
2. False
3. False
4. True
5. False
6. True
7. True

ANSWERS TO TEST ON THE OUR FATHER
(p. 458)

Completion:

1. (a) perfect; (b) unselfish
2. (a) Christ; (b) Apostles
3. (a) soul; (b) body or physical and spiritual life
4. honor
5. (a) body; (b) soul
6. as we forgive those who trespass against us

ANSWERS TO END OF UNIT TESTS FOR UNIT FIVE, SECTIONS I, II, III (Text, pp. 460–461)

I. Multiple Choice (p. 460):

1. C
2. C
3. D
4. B
5. C
6. D
7. B
8. C
9. B
10. C

II. True — False (p. 461):

1. False
2. True
3. False
4. True
5. False

III. Recognition (p. 461):

1. sacrament
2. sacramental
3. sacramental
4. sacrament
5. sacramental
6. sacramental
7. sacrament
8. sacrament
9. sacramental
10. sacrament

MEMORY BOX

Can you name the following:

The 3 things that make sin mortal?
The 4 marks of the Church?
The 4 Gospels?
The 7 gifts of the Holy Ghost?
The 10 Commandments?
The 3 main parts of the Mass?
The 6 Precepts of the Church?
The 6 holydays of obligation in the United States?
The 7 Sacraments?
The 3 Theological Virtues?
The 3 Evangelical Counsels?
The 4 Cardinal Virtues?
The 5 Joyful Mysteries of the Rosary?
The 5 Sorrowful Mysteries of the Rosary?
The 5 Glorious Mysteries of the Rosary?
The 7 Capital Sins?
The 8 Beatitudes?

The 5 things for a good confession?
The 12 Fruits of the Holy Ghost?
The 14 Stations of the Cross?
The 7 Sorrows of the Blessed Virgin Mary?
The 7 last words of our Lord on the cross?
The 12 Apostles?
The 7 Corporal Works of Mercy?
The 7 Spiritual Works of Mercy?

REFERENCES AND MATERIALS

UNIT FIVE — SANCTIFICATION THROUGH THE SACRAMENTALS AND PRAYERS

A. Pupil References

Fitzpatrick, Edward A., *The Highway to God* (Milwaukee: Bruce, 1942).

Hornback, Florence M., *When We Say "Our Father"* (Paterson, N. J.: St. Anthony Guild).

———— *When We Say "Hail Mary"* (Paterson, N. J.: St. Anthony Guild).

B. Teacher References

Baierl, Rev. Joseph J., *Grace and Prayer Explained* (Rochester, N. Y.: Seminary Press).

Christopher, J., and Spence, *The Raccolta* (New York: Benziger).

Cavanagh, Rev. William J., *A Manual for Teachers of Religion* (Milwaukee: Bruce, 1951).

Connell, Rev. Francis J., *New Baltimore Catechism No. 3*, Official Revised Edition (New York: Benziger).

Drinkwater, Rev. F. H., *Catechism Stories* (Westminster: Newman Press, 1948).

Gasquet, *Sacramentals and Some Catholic Practices* (St. Paul, Minn.: Lohmann).

Heeg, Rev. Aloysius J., *How to Teach the Sacraments*, Part VI (St. Louis: Queen's Work).

Horan, Ellamay, *Handbook for Teachers of Religion in Grades 6, 7, 8* (New York: Sadlier, 1945, 1947).

Kelly, Very Rev. Msgr. W. R., Goebel, Rev. Edmund J., and Schumacher, Rt. Rev. Msgr. M. A., *Living Through God's Gifts* (New York: Benziger).

Lambing, Rev. A. A., *The Sacramentals of the Holy Catholic Church* (New York: Benziger).

O'Rafferty, Rev. Nicholas, *Instruction on Christian Doctrine* (Milwaukee: Bruce, 1940).

Perkins, Mary, *Speaking of How to Pray* (New York: Sheed & Ward).

Schumacher, Msgr. M. A., *How to Teach the Catechism*, Vol. III (New York: Benziger, 1946).

Spirago, Rev. Francis, and Baxter, Rev. James J., *Anecdotes and Examples for the Catechism* (New York: Benziger, 1904).

Spirago, Rev. Francis, and Clarke, Rev. Richard F., *The Catechism Explained* (New York: Benziger, 1921).

Strugnell, Rev. Joseph, *When Ye Pray, Pray Ye Thus* (Paterson, N. J.: St. Anthony Guild Press).

C. Materials (Audio-Visual Aids)

CHARTS:

Prayer Charts, two charts: 22 by 28. Catechetical Guild, Educational Society, St. Paul 2, Minn.

FILMSTRIPS:

Prayer No. 836, Exposition of nature and importance of prayer, etc., Catechetical Guild.

Hail Mary, No. 837, Catechetical Guild.

Rosary Meditations, 69 frames Audio-Visual Devotional Filmstrip and four 12″ Record Albums. Cath. Visual Ed., Inc., Chicago, Ill.

Way of the Cross, 18 frames, Catholic Visual Ed.

Sacramentals and Indulgences, No. 808, Catechetical Guild.

Prayer and Its Kinds, No. 843, Catechetical Guild.

The Our Father and Other Prayers, No. 844. Catechetical Guild.

RECORDINGS:

Record No. 1046, Catholic Prayers, Halligan Audio-Visual Studio, 475 Fifth Avenue, New York 17, N. Y.

CPSIA information can be obtained
at www.ICGtesting.com
Printed in the USA
JSHW021232200220
4329JS00002B/6